The
Best Is Yet
to Come

Books by Ivana Trump

For Love Alone
Free to Love
The Best Is Yet to Come

Published by POCKET BOOKS

The Best Is Yet to Come

Coping with Divorce and Enjoying Life Again

Ivana Trump

POCKET BOOKS

New York   London   Toronto   Sydney   Tokyo   Singapore

POCKET BOOKS, a division of Simon & Schuster Inc.
1230 Avenue of the Americas, New York, NY 10020

Trump, Ivana.
 ، The best is yet to come: coping with divorce and enjoying life
again / Ivana Trump.
        p.   cm.
    ISBN 0-671-86569-2
    1. Divorce—Psychological aspects.   2. Divorced women—Life skills
guides. I. Title.
HQ814.T78   1995
    306.89—dc20   94-31889
                                                          CIP

First Pocket Books hardcover printing May 1995

10 9 8 7 6 5 4 3 2

Printed in the U.S.A.

This book is dedicated to all the women who supported me in my difficult times. For their letters, postcards, prayers, benedictions, shared tears, hopes, and dreams. For all of this I am grateful.

I would like to give special thanks to Penina Spiegel for her dedication, insight, and hard work, which helped make this book what I hoped it would be.

Note

Names of acquaintances marked with an asterisk (*) have been changed.

I remembered hearing something about an ex-wife being the most pathetic creature on earth, somebody only fit to slink off into the shadows. Well, I thought, we'll just see about that.

—*Ivana Trump*

Contents

Contents

Contents

plained our breakup to my children • Donald, Jr., defends my honor; Ivanka rides the wave; Eric is distracted • Don't knock your ex to the kids • But what if he's *really* rotten? • Coparenting and joint custody • How to manage the "control freak" • Making visitations work: Be the good guy for your kids' sake • In-laws and relatives

Contents

Contents

When and how to bring your new man home to meet the kids • What if they hate him? • When you or your spouse remarries and has other children • When my children's father remarried • Safe sex or no sex • Tips for a man who is dating a newly single woman

Part 5
The Best Is Yet to Come

Mix up a big batch of love, fun, discipline, manners, sports, languages—and talk, talk, talk! • "Help! My 'baby' is going out on dates!" • Talking to kids about contraception • Drugs, drinking, driving, early pregnancy, marriage • Teach your sons to treat women the way you would like men to treat you

Learn to be socially graceful • Use the skills you already have for a better life • All the wonderful things that have happened to me that wouldn't have if I'd still been married • Dream big dreams and make them come true

Foreword

No bride ever walks down the aisle thinking about divorce. It's the furthest thing from your mind; we women are far too romantic for that. What little girl can't tell you all about the wedding she will have one day? She knows every detail: what she'll wear, what her bridesmaids will wear, the flowers, the music, and of course, the handsome groom.

I was no different. When I married Donald I believed with all my heart that this marriage, these vows we were taking, would be for ever and always. Sure, I'd heard the statistics. I knew as well as anyone how many marriages end in divorce. But who ever thinks they will apply to her?

I didn't.

I loved Donald, and he loved me. That was all that mattered.

I couldn't have been more wrong, could I? Not only did my marriage break up, every moment of it was reported in the press and on television around the world.

1

If the last thing I wanted was for my marriage to break up, the *absolute* last thing in the universe I wanted was to have it explode in the public eye.

Things happen, don't they? What's that expression— "Man proposes and God disposes." Some things are out of our control.

Maybe *because* it was all so public, so many of you put pen to paper and wrote me. I got thousands of letters, from all over the country, many from foreign lands. Nuns wrote to say they were praying for me. Muslim fakirs wrote offering to hypnotize Donald into obeying me. Grandmothers wrote to convey blessings; entire offices got together to let me know of their support and good wishes. I heard from teenagers and schoolchildren.

But by far the greatest number of my correspondents were women; many of them had been through or were going through a divorce themselves. They shared their stories; they were generous with words of support, of sympathy and encouragement.

> I never write letters to people I don't know, yet I feel I know you. I can't help but think I know some of the pain and heartache you are feeling. My husband and I separated and I remember so vividly the pain I felt—and my divorce was nine years ago!
>
> Monica

> I have always thought of you and Mr. Trump as America's Prince and Princess. We all need some fantasy in our lives and you were my fantasy. When I heard about your breakup, I was devastated. I felt like a child who had been told there was no Santa Claus.
>
> Laura

> Dear Ivana, I really feel for what you are going through. It makes me sad when I see all that stuff on TV and in

the papers. I myself am just a young housewife with three children and I look up to you as a role model.

Miriam

These were letters from people I never met, who never met me! It meant so much, at a very difficult time in my life. Their message, that I was not alone, was very comforting.

There are very obvious and very important differences in our lives—I don't minimize the financial gulf between us—but these women are able to see past them.

Yes, I live in a town house and spend my weekends in a country mansion. I travel by limousines, private jets, or yacht. I can buy just about anything I want. When you see me out for the evening, attending some ball or charity function, you see a smiling, glamorous woman. My hair and nails are immaculate. My gown bears the name of a famous designer.

But that's all surface. Monica knew how I felt; so did Laura and Miriam. They saw past the gleam and the glamour to the heart of the matter: Every divorce is a tragedy. It's a death—the demise of the future you two envisioned having together, the end of a dream.

Whether you're rich or poor, you get married intending to make a happy life with your husband till death do you part. And when it doesn't work out that way, you can't help but know that you have failed in something that was very important to you.

Ida

Ida is right. It is better to have money than not, but it's no shield against the awful emotions that overwhelm you when your marriage breaks up: the pain, the humiliation, the fear and the sense of failure. These feelings are universal.

True, I don't have to worry where my next meal is coming from, but I spent plenty of nights wondering what was going to happen to me and my kids. I cried plenty of tears. No matter how much money you have, the trauma affects you in exactly the same way, and it takes you just as long to recover.

The breakup of my marriage was very nearly the worst thing that ever happened to me. I felt terribly defeated, as if I had failed everyone: my children, my husband, myself. It broke my parents' hearts, especially my dear father's.

Some women write me that when their marriage broke up, they had thoughts of suicide. I myself never felt that way. The thought never entered my mind. I like life too much. Also, what would my children do? Divorce is bad enough, what would it do to them to lose their mother? This is the time when they need her the most!

But don't think I wasn't afraid. My particular horror was the unknown. I plan as far ahead as I can. I like to know what's going to happen. Of course I could, God forbid, become ill or get run over by a truck; that's unforeseen. But whatever is in my control I've got planned. I know exactly what I want to achieve by the end of this year, what I'd like to have happen by the end of next year, and the year after. And five years from now.

And here I was, faced with the unknown: What will happen to me and my children? Will their father hire a barracuda lawyer and have us cast out of our home? Of course nothing like that happened, but when your marriage crashes around you, you tend to see things very darkly. And I knew things like that do happen, so you can't tell yourself it's out of the realm of possibility.

At the time my ex-husband and I separated, I was president of the Plaza Hotel, but I knew that I wouldn't be for too much longer. It would be better for all concerned if I didn't continue to work for my newly ex-husband. But what would I do? I'm not a woman who can stand to be without work. I go crazy any time I'm not overbooked, overscheduled, overworked, and overloaded.

The breakup of my marriage was not the very worst thing that ever happened to me. I lost my fiancé in a car crash when I was just twenty-one. The death of a young man with a brilliant future, whom you just happen to love, is very hard to bear.

But the divorce was surely the second hardest thing that had ever come to me. I walked around feeling sad for a long time; and when I think about it, I'm still sad.

However, even at my lowest point, I had a certain confidence in myself. I knew that I wasn't going to be alone: I have three beautiful, healthy children—my real treasures. I knew I wasn't going to be destitute. I wouldn't be out on the street. I had some money put aside, and I knew I was capable of working very hard. I told myself that even if I had to be a saleslady this year, I'd be head of merchandising next year. And the year after, maybe I'd own my own store.

None of my dire middle-of-the-night fears came true. But it's safe to say that my wildest dreams did. Today I'm a writer and a clothing and jewelry designer. I have speaking engagements all over the country—and lots more things in the works, including a line of accessories and Ivana cosmetics. By the time this book is in your hands, Ivana perfume will be available for you to enjoy.

I can honestly say that I'm better off now than I was before. Being on my own allowed me to move in new directions, to develop new resources and new ways of expressing myself. I'm stronger and more confident now than I was when I was married. After all, the worst happened—I'm divorced, and I'm still here. I've survived. Better than that, I've flourished. If my marriage hadn't broken up I probably would never have explored the wonderful new avenues I'm following now.

My life didn't end when my marriage did; in fact, it became much richer and more purposeful.

I don't stand in anyone's shadow anymore.

At the time my marriage broke up I would have sworn I'd never get involved with another man as long as I lived. It's a good thing I didn't take any oaths, because there is romance in my life today. I believe very firmly that having a man to be with makes life much sweeter. Of course, it takes a while after your divorce for you even to *think* of romance. But as they say, time does heal, and as far as I'm concerned, one sign of healing is being able to allow a special man into your life and enjoy the pleasure and excitement and the champagne-bubble feeling that he brings to you.

So maybe it was all for the best. All the heartache and the pain. Maybe the way to think of it is as a rebirth. Nobody said giving birth is easy, but there's no other way to get the job done, is there?

If you had told me during my dark times that I would one day feel this way . . . I wonder whether I would have believed you.

And you, reading this right now, you may not believe *me*. That's why I'm writing this book.

Wherever I go, when I give speeches or sign books, women always come up to me and ask me, how did I get from there to here? They remember the dark days when the newspapers presented me daily as "a woman scorned." And here I am, better than ever. How'd I do it? What was my secret?

That's what I'm going to tell you—not just how *I* did it, how others did as well. I've spoken to experts and to friends. I've gathered some of their stories and some of mine. I'll share with you stories from women who wrote to me.

I'll tell you many things you need to know; how many of us felt, and how you may expect to feel. We'll cover it from the very beginning, when you begin to get an inkling that your marriage is breaking up. I'll help you decide whether to try and repair your marriage or give it up and start again.

I'll tell you many practical things that people usually don't pass along. Not just how to hire a divorce lawyer but *exactly* what to say when you walk into his office, what questions to ask and what traps to avoid. The same with accountants, brokers, plastic surgeons, nutritionists, physical trainers—even auto mechanics.

We'll talk about looking your best—about your physical and mental health. And how to cope with your changed lifestyle.

We'll talk about social life, dating, romance, and sex.

And children. Children are very important to me. Mine I absolutely treasure, of course, but because I'm a mother it matters very much to me how other children survive divorce. I believe there are many ways you can help them, and we have a lengthy chapter on children in this book.

Now I know that the women in my circle have far more money to spend than the average reader will. But just as the emotions that are involved in divorce are the same, so are many of the suggestions that will help you, and in every case I've included several options that are not expensive. If you can afford to spend your first Christmas alone at a spa, on a cruise, or in Vienna, marvelous. But I have plenty of ideas for the woman who couldn't possibly afford those things.

I'm going to give you a lot of my own opinions and sometimes those of my friends. They make sense to me; maybe they will to you too.

Some people accuse me of being pro-woman. Guilty! I'm a woman, who else should I be "pro"? However, being for women does not mean being anti-man. Heaven forbid! No one adores those magnificent creatures more than I. I need and want men in my life: a special one to love, my two sons whom I cherish, other male friends. I do feel, though, that men start out with so many extra advantages, and certainly when it comes to divorce they usually have the money and the power—they don't need Ivana to defend them and speak for them.

One thing I know for sure. It *is* possible to build a new life after divorce. I firmly believe that you can make your life after divorce far better than it was before—better than you could have hoped for if you had stayed married. Yes, you're going to have to work very hard. You're going to need a support system. But you're going to make it. I believe that.

I wish I had some kind of magic wand that would protect you against the breakup of a marriage and loss of a spouse. But since I don't, this is the next-best thing.

Part 1

The Beginning
of the End

Chapter 1

Watching for the Warning Signs

I don't think any marriage ever ends on impulse. It may come as a surprise to one of you, but you can bet the other one has been planning it for a long time. Still, so many women write me that they had no idea of what was coming; the husband's announcement or the discovery of his affair seemed to come out of the blue.

You've heard that expression, "The wife is the last to know." Well, I'm here to try to change that. I believe you'll be far better off if you're prepared for what's coming. I learned the hard way, and so did many of the women who wrote to me. More than one marriage has exploded in the wife's face and she never had an inkling that anything was wrong!

How can this happen? Well, some men are just very good cheats. They come home at 6 P.M., never miss an evening at home. There are no odd, unexplained nights out with the boys . . . but they fool around during the day. The wife may not catch on until he gets careless, and there are men who can go quite a while without getting careless. By then it might be too late since he may be very attached to the new woman and probably doesn't care anymore if he gets caught.

Let's say you notice that he doesn't make love with you as much as he did. But it's so easy to understand, when you look at the kind of pressure he's under at work—and in recent times so many people have had difficulties. Of *course* you accept without question that he's tired. And even if it crosses your mind to wonder, you don't rush out to hire a private detective because you've gone three months without sex—especially because in your heart of hearts you want so much to believe in him.

And he certainly *helps* you maintain your belief in him. He *works* at it. He doesn't say, "I haven't touched you because I'm getting all the sex I need with my lover." No! Instead, he'll say something like, "I know I'm not paying enough attention to you, and I'm so sorry about it, but I'm having financial problems." He's wearing himself out holding the family's financial assets together . . . how can you do *other* than believe him? So you try extra hard not to put any extra pressure on him. Doesn't he have enough on his shoulders as it is?

Or if you go to him and say, "Darling, do you know we haven't made love in fourteen days?" Trust me, he won't say, "It's because I'm in love with another woman." He'll say, "It's just that I'm struggling through this very bad period. It'll be over soon and I'll make it up to you. I promise."

And so you suspect nothing. Until you find a little love note to him that you didn't write . . . or pick up the phone to make a call and overhear him talking love talk to Her. Or, as in my case, a woman you have never laid eyes on before comes up to you—virtually out of a clear blue sky—and announces herself and her presence in his life.

I had no idea that anything was amiss in my marriage. Cindy Adams, the columnist, came over to me at a charity dinner at the Waldorf Astoria and said something like, "Ivana, are you *all right*? Is everything *all right* with you and Donald? Is he behaving himself?"

I said, "Of course. Why do you ask?"

Looking back, I wonder if she had heard rumors and was trying to tell me something. But until the situation exploded on the ski slopes of Aspen, I have to count myself as one of the wives who didn't suspect anything.

I'd been married for six years when my husband walked in one day and announced he wanted a divorce. That was all he said. He went upstairs, packed, and left. I immediately thought it was something I did, something about me. I begged him to tell me what it was, and I'd change it. I cried, "How can I be different if I don't know what to change?"

Frances

My husband left me and our two small children four days after Christmas. Without any warning, he never said a word. He was just up and gone. I had no idea he was going to do this.

Eva

Frances's husband didn't decide, suddenly, on the commuter train back to the suburbs, to end their marriage. And Eva's husband's departure wasn't sudden at all. He waited until after Christmas so as not to ruin the children's holiday. When you think about it, it's obvious, isn't it?

The signs are there. Almost always. We just don't allow ourselves to see them.

We don't do it on purpose. We women are so busy trying to be all things to all people. Nowadays it's not enough to be a lady in the living room, a prostitute in the bedroom, and a madonna in the nursery, we also have to be an executive in the office. It's hard switching gears from "tough competitor" to "nurturing housewife" just because you've left the office.

And when we do get home, what takes priority? The most immediate things cry out—dinner has to be on the table, homework done, and children bathed. Who has time or energy to keep track of our *own* emotional needs, let alone our husband's?

So what holds our marriages together? Let's face it, the incredible passion and desire of the early days of the romance eventually fade no matter what, so it certainly isn't a constant mad desire to make love that keeps most married couples together.

If you're lucky, you become each other's best friend and special confidant. But too often the couple become like partners in a business venture, the business consisting of their home and children. They meet to exchange information, and each goes his own way.

And one day, you may find yourself glancing over at the person sleeping next to you and wondering who he is and how he came to be in your bed.

I think that's a dangerous state to get into. You owe it to yourself to keep alert to what's going on with your marriage. The vibrations are out there; you have to be willing to receive them.

Whoever said ignorance is bliss never went through a divorce. I have. And I can tell you, the more you know the better off you are. You can think, you can prepare, you can act. In short, you can take care of yourself and your children who depend on you.

Noted New York City matrimonial lawyer Ira Garr has a lot of experience with broken marriages. He says, "People often think the affair comes before the breakup of the marriage. I sometimes think it's the other way around, that something faltered in the marriage, and that led a person who otherwise may not have been interested in an affair to look elsewhere. I'm not saying that's always the case. A guy who's always been a womanizer might have run around throughout the marriage never intending to leave, until he meets one woman who really hits it for him. But very often you have a couple who both really wanted a monogamous relationship, but something wasn't happening at home for one of them.

"Take it from the top: Two people get married. The husband's in medical school, they're living on a shoestring budget. The wife is working. She sees him when he's up late studying. She sees him when he has the flu, when his nose is running. They've known each other since they were college kids.

"Ah, but now he's a doctor, a famous surgeon. He's making two million dollars a year and every day he goes to the hospital where he's treated like a king. Everybody asks his opinion. Everybody wants to know what he thinks about world affairs. After all, he's a doctor, he must know.

"He comes home to his wife and to her he's the same boy he was when they married. He doesn't look any different to her—if anything, he was a lot cuter then. He says, 'Do you have dinner for me?' She says, 'Nah, let's order in.'

"Everybody caters to him except his wife. Believe me, he's beginning to feel a little underappreciated. And when he feels unappreciated, he becomes susceptible. He meets some woman who says to him, 'You know, you've got the greenest eyes I've ever seen?' and all of a sudden, he feels fifteen again. He's being *courted!*

"He goes home to his wife, she says, 'Honey, take out the trash.' *She* doesn't think about his eyes.

"So now he's thinking about the woman who marveled at his eyes, his sensitive hands. He's still thinking about

15

her the next day. Maybe he gives her a call. And before you know it, he may be out of the marriage.

"It works the other way, too: As many women want out of the marriage as men. It's the exact same syndrome in reverse. You meet somebody, marry her, she's a lovely wife and mother. But you take her for granted. Valentine's Day comes. Do you bring roses? Maybe, maybe not. Her birthday comes . . . Oops. Well, you'll make it up to her. Christmas—you get something, sure. But do you ever just come home with some flowers? You don't do it. It doesn't even cross your mind. You come home and say, 'The expressway was murder, I'm starved.'

"I have guys tell me, 'As soon as I got separated and started to date, I'd send roses, I'd send a limousine, I'd do wonderful things. I realized I was treating strangers better than I treated my wife!'

"But of course by then it's too late."

You tell yourself a million different things in order to keep yourself from knowing the truth. Is your man polishing himself up lately? Has he lost a lot of weight? Is he working out in the gym? Has he taken a sudden interest in his clothes? And most important . . . has he stopped sleeping with you? If he has, my dear, unless he has a very minimal sex drive, you have to wonder if he's sleeping with someone else.

Let's say you do pick up on those vibes and you get the feeling your mate is becoming restless, but your marriage has not yet reached the breaking point. Is there anything you can do to stop the marriage from coming apart?

Possibly.

You can try to be your husband's mistress. If he already has a new girlfriend, it's probably too late. But if not, and you really give him the royal treatment, your marriage will have new life. It may or may not work, but I know

16

of cases where it did, and it's certainly worth a try. One of my friends managed to save her marriage in just this way: by giving her husband a lot of special attention. If you want to go this route, a good thing to do is to take him away someplace romantic—just the two of you. Leave the kids with your mother, or a friend. (You can trade this favor with your friend. Give her a chance to go off with her husband while you watch her kids.) Or hire a sitter to stay with the children. You might know a college girl, or perhaps a niece or the daughter of a friend who would be happy to make a few extra dollars. Often young people enjoy spending the weekend with children, doing kid stuff: fingerpainting, baking, going to the zoo, whatever. If you have someone like this in your circle, probably your children already know and like him or her. (There's nothing wrong with a male student for your boys—as a matter of fact, I like it. They'll have great fun together and he can be their role model.) Whatever arrangements you have to make—make them. It'll be worth it if you can save your marriage (if, in fact, that's what you want to do).

It might well be that all your husband needs is a little more petting and a little less criticism; warm arms instead of a cold shoulder. After all, isn't that what a mistress does? She fusses over him and tells him how smart he is, how great he looks?

If he returns to you emotionally, your marriage will have new life, and that will benefit you, too. If a man is bored and numbed by the routine, what kind of a husband and lover can he be to *you?*

However, if he already has a new girlfriend, it's probably too late.

I have a friend, we'll call her Charlotte* because you'd know her name if I told it to you. Charlotte is a darling woman—elegant, accomplished, successful in a competitive career. I don't know why a man who had her would look elsewhere, and I guess she felt the same way because

17

her husband's fidelity was not something she worried about. She's very hardworking, so she doesn't have time to shop much, but one day as her limousine was passing Martha's, then a very exclusive boutique on Park Avenue, she spotted a beautiful Chanel gown in the window. There was a charity ball coming up and she thought, why not? She had her driver pull over, went into the shop, and asked if they had the gown in the window in a size six.

What happened next would never have happened if Martha or her daughter Lynn had been there, but at this moment there was only a saleswoman. The saleswoman told her that the gown in the window had just been sold— she hadn't had time to take it off display, but she'd check in the back and see if she had another. She found the dress and it fit perfectly. Charlotte charged it to her personal checking account. Why drive her very wealthy husband crazy with a bill for six thousand dollars for one dress? The saleswoman looked at the check. "What a coincidence," she said. "The woman who bought the other dress—the one in the window—had the same name as yours. Another Mrs. X! And she charged it to your husband's store account."

Charlotte covered her shock. She murmured something about a large family, many aunts and cousins, all of whom shopped at Martha's.

"Oh dear," said the saleswoman. "I hope you weren't planning to wear it to the opening of the American Ballet Theater, because the other Mrs. X mentioned to me *she* was going to wear it there."

That was *exactly* what Charlotte had in mind.

She took the dress home and said nothing to her husband. On the night of the ball, she wore the dress. And she kept a sharp eye out for the other "Mrs. X," whom she'd know because they were wearing the same gown. Sure enough, as she and her husband are in the receiving line, she turns and looks at the new arrivals and sees her

18

dress. "Look at that," she tells her husband. "There's a woman wearing the same dress as me."

Without missing a beat, he says: "It looks a thousand times better on you, darling." The swine!

And that's how Charlotte found out that her husband was carrying on a little amour on the side. Not so little, actually. If he's buying her Chanel gowns, the romance is probably very entrenched.

Charlotte didn't let on that anything was wrong. She waited until the woman got up to go to the dance floor. Then she made an excuse to leave her table, casually swept by the other woman's seat, and glanced at the place card.

Now at least she knew the name. It was odd that she didn't know the woman by sight; usually we all know each other.

Charlotte still didn't confront her husband. Instead, she made plans. She knew that she wouldn't be able to go on living with the man now that she knew he was lying to her and cheating on her. She wanted out of her marriage. For her, as for me, trust means more than money or fame. But she wanted to make sure her interests would be protected before she left.

A paper trail undoes many heretofore secret extramarital affairs. In wealthy circles often it is the custom for the wife to have various charge accounts around town for which she never sees the bills. They go directly to the husband's office and are paid from there. The wife may even forget that bills exist—something a woman less well off could never do—and that may be her undoing. For not only do they exist, they can often tell tales.

My friend Reggie* was checking over his household bills, and he noticed that the limousine service charges had jumped in the past few months. His wife was ordering limos more often than she used to, and when he examined the charges, he saw that she ordered limos on the same day of the week, and at the same time.

Since she had her own car and driver, he wondered why she was using a service. So on the next Monday at three or whatever, he planted himself outside his home, watched the limo pick her up, and followed it. After she went in, he waited a few minutes and then surprised his wife and her (married) lover at a very, shall we say, inconvenient moment. That marriage blew up with quite a scandal.

Of course you're wondering, Why *did* Reggie's wife use a limousine service if she had her own car and driver? Because she was trying to be discreet, of course. But she forgot about those nasty little bills. Oops.

There's another story that made the rounds, which made us all absolutely scream with laughter. A woman I know had always hankered for a sable coat. Well, you're talking sixty to a hundred thousand dollars, so her husband wasn't that keen on it. No matter how hard she hinted, no sable coat was forthcoming, until one glorious Christmas morning when she opened a large box to find the coat of her dreams. She put it on; it fit perfectly. She covered his face with kisses. She twirled away to see how the coat hung . . . and caught sight in the mirror of the name embroidered in the lining. Needless to say, it wasn't hers, but HERS.

The man had ordered the coat sent to his mistress. The shipping clerk, recognizing the name on the sales slip, didn't bother to check the "ship to" but merely sent it directly on to the buyer's home. Which is how the sable wound up in the "wrong" hands.

It's just as the song says: It really is "a small, small world"—especially if you travel in certain circles. Basically, in my crowd we all attend the same functions, dine in the same restaurants, use the same caterers and florists, shop in the same stores. My friend Janet's* husband traveled back and forth to Los Angeles on business very frequently. Janet was lunching at Le Cirque one day when one of her girlfriends mentioned that she'd run into Janet's husband more than once in a certain posh jewelry store on Rodeo Drive in Beverly Hills. The woman said that he'd picked out several lovely pieces to surprise Janet with and she was sure Janet had quite a collection by now.

Hmmm. Needless to say, Janet was not on the receiving end of these goodies. She said nothing. Instead, she took a little trip to Los Angeles herself, went from the airport to the store, and struck up a conversation with one of the salesladies. Janet invited her to lunch, where, in exchange for a cash "gift," the saleswoman told her who was getting all the expensive jewelry that Janet's husband was buying.

Janet caught a plane home that same day, got herself a lawyer, and confronted her husband. She got a huge settlement when they divorced.

I'm always surprised when I find out women are cheating on their husbands. To me it seems more likely to be the other way around. But you do hear of it every once in a while, maybe more so in recent years than used to be the case. When we were chatting about it recently, my friend Nikki Haskell pointed out that a woman has the advantage because her day is her own and she basically doesn't have to account for anything. All the husband wants to know is that when he comes home, the kids are fed and dinner is on the table. She can fake it from nine in the morning till six at night. Because he usually works, a man can sneak around only between lunch and dinner or fake an evening business meeting.

I suppose the lesson is that no matter what your sex, if you think you have cause to worry about your spouse's fidelity . . . you probably do.

The Best Is Yet to Come

Divorce attorney Ira Garr claims he sees as many women as men being unfaithful. "When a man asks me, 'My wife spends three hours a day in the supermarket, should I be worried?' I always say yes. Any change in behavior could be a tip-off. It could be nothing, but it could also be that one clue that will tell you what's going on."

And sometimes it can be the strangest, smallest thing. Something you never would have thought of in a million years. There's a story that has become legend in social circles, about a woman who was married to a very prominent man. She met someone else and began a clandestine extramarital affair. They were very careful, never met in the same hotel room twice. So how did the husband manage to walk in on them, in flagrante delicto, as they say?

Her maid, who was *his* maid before their marriage, happened to notice that the wife had put an extra pair of panties in her handbag as she was getting ready to leave the house that day. Why this should have set off alarm bells I don't know (since I've never had an illicit affair and I never had to think through the need for fresh panties in hotel rooms), but the maid thought enough of this "clue" to call the husband at work. He immediately had someone tail his wife when she left the house, and when she met her sweetie for their rendezvous, the detective called the husband to come over—just in time to catch the amorous couple in the act.

The husband divorced her. She's spent the better part of the last few years trying to get her husband back, but he won't have any part of it—he can't trust her anymore.

There are certain rules to this game of marriage that you can never break, because if you do, it stops everything dead in its tracks. I think you should think twice before cheating on your husband.

Ah, but what if you've fallen in love with somebody else?

It does happen, I know. Still, you have to be a lady. Somehow you have to find a way to be honest with your spouse. What you want to avoid at all costs is a situation in which your spouse will find out indirectly, from somebody else. Let's face it—if you have managed to fall in love with someone new, you must be spending *some* time together. And if so, chances are someone will spot you one of these days. Yes, I know you're very careful. Nevertheless, the odds are against you.

Sometimes it seems to me that the partner who's cheating doesn't even make an effort to keep it from his/her spouse. It's as if they don't care anymore. That's sad ... and degrading, it seems to me. I know a case where the wife, who had inherited money, went to Paris for the couture collections and took her lover with her. Now, the top designers' fashion shows probably draw more press than anything but a royal wedding. So of course, the next day, the husband opens his morning paper and reads in one of the columns that his wife and her lover were seen kissing and canoodling at Dior's or wherever.

That's a dismal way for someone to find out that his spouse is involved with somebody else. It makes the wife seem nothing but a cheat.

And yet, she must have known she'd be found out. She's not stupid; every photographer in the world is in Paris for the collections. She may have hoped that her husband would simply turn a blind eye; people sometimes do. But I strongly believe that if you've fallen in love with somebody else, you must at least give your spouse the courtesy of hearing it from you. Not from the paper, not from the neighbor. From your own mouth. I'm not saying it would be the easiest news to break, but I'm afraid it's absolutely necessary. I think it's just awful to wait until somebody else tells him—and they will.

What could you say to him? Well, maybe something like: "Dear, I fell in love with a man whom I adore and

I don't want to be cheating behind your back. Maybe we should separate for a couple of months and then we'll reevaluate, see what's what."

If he (or she) agrees, maybe you'll find your marriage wasn't serving your needs and you really want to be with your new man. Or, just maybe, you'll find out the grass is no greener anywhere else, you've just been forgetting to water your own lawn.

Chapter 2

Preparing for the Breakup

*Y*ou discover your husband has been unfaith-ful or otherwise impossible. Now you have a decision to make. Do you stay in the marriage and try to make it work, or do you strike out on your own?

I've had many letters from women who discovered their husbands were cheating on them and took them back, for one reason or another. Sometimes it's for the children, sometimes it's because they're afraid to be alone. If you decide you don't want to leave, can't leave, or are afraid to leave, you will then have to learn to live with a man while knowing that he is unfaithful.

I've tried to tolerate fifteen years of infidelity. If I had economic security I would file for separation.

Ginny

25

Knowing I'm stuck in a no-longer-functioning relationship, yet not having the resources to get out, is terrible
for me. I only stay so I can have a roof over my head.

Audrey

Some women feel that what they have in the marriage
is more important than what they don't have. There's a
certain society grande dame whose husband has had a
mistress for twenty-five years. The wife has the jewelry
and the money and the balls and dinners, and if the mistress has his heart, I guess the wife has learned to live
without it. One thing's for sure, she's not about to give
up all the jewelry, the money, etc., etc., etc. So they stay
together. For all I know, she's reached the point where
she no longer cares what he's doing as long as he's there
when she needs him and he's wearing the appropriate
clothing.

Often the man knows that his wife feels this way, and
he comes to count on it. He can have his fling, then come
back, and the wife will go on as if nothing happened. He
does it once . . . he does it twice . . . and the pattern is set.
Maybe she will cry and storm but he'll buy her a terrific
jewel and things will settle down just the way they were
before.

Until the next time.

And in his mind, he's not really cheating. He always
comes back, doesn't he? Cheating would be if he risked
his marriage. And clearly, his marriage isn't at risk.

It seems to me if you care the least little bit for the
other person, then living with an arrangement like that
would be pure hell. I simply could not tolerate it—but
obviously some women can and do.

Take Betsy,* for example.

Before I married Donald, I lived in Montreal, Canada,
and on weekends I was a ski instructor and junior team
coach to make extra money. My boyfriend at the time was

26

an excellent skier, and we'd go with a group of friends to Jay Peak every weekend where we'd chip in and rent a chalet. There were about sixteen of us and one was a girl called Betsy. She was a little plain but nice and giggly and fun to be with.

Our paths separated, I moved to New York, got married. And eventually divorced. Until my divorce was final, I didn't even look at a man, but then when I was finally a free agent I met a man who started to romance me. We went dancing a few times. We talked about my being divorced, but he presented himself as single. The man in question was doing a business deal with a man whose wife is one of my best girlfriends. I saw him in their house socially all the time and he was very handsome and kind and successful.

When my girlfriend found out we had been dating, she said, "Ivana, do you know that he's got this girl?"

I said, "Every man has a girl."

"This is different. He has a home with her. And a child."

That *is* different.

She went on: "He's lived with her for twelve years. But I think you know her because she says she knows you."

The moment my friend said the name, of course I knew who she was. You guessed it—the girl was Betsy. It really *is* a small world, isn't it?

When I heard this, I confronted him. Why on earth didn't he marry the girl? She'd been with him for twelve years. She gave him a son. He must feel something for her.

His answer was that he wasn't sure he wanted to marry. Now here's a case of a man who could claim to be "single"—technically. He hadn't married anybody. So he could go on trips and date whomever he pleased. Instead of having a mistress on the side, he had a *wife on the side*.

I found it so dishonest that I wouldn't go out with him

27

anymore. And I wondered about the girl. Why would she allow this? Betsy must love him enough to stick with him in the hope that he will marry her one day.

But why is he so tied to her? What's been keeping him with her all these years without benefit of law or ceremony?

It's very simple. When he met Betsy, this man wasn't really very wealthy. He went on to become a very successful banker with gorgeous homes in London and Montreal. He built a beautiful yacht, had the Falconer 900 jet—all the toys. Then his company got into trouble and he went bankrupt. But Betsy stuck with him, through thin as well as thick. She loved him poor, she loved him rich, she loved him poor again—and she loved him rich again, for he's since made back his money.

That's the tie between them. This man is no fool. He knows that when he's in the money, he could have many women. But Betsy wanted him even when he had nothing. He can be sure that she's not with him for his money. There are a lot of fortune hunters out there and the men are very careful.

Although I'm still friends with this man, I never went out with him again. I told him if I go out with somebody and I start a relationship it has to be a *real* relationship.

I do not condone nor accept this behavior, but I am old enough to realize why it exists. Most men are the same in their lustful desires, and if you leave this one, who's to say your next spouse will be faithful? Twenty years ago I told my husband that if he ever cheated there would be no divorce, just death. Now that I'm older and wiser, I say to myself, if he ever betrayed me I would not let it destroy my marriage, my life, and break up my happy home. Why should I lose all that I worked for and give it to some other woman?

Lucille

You see, different women react differently. The trick is to find the approach that works for you. Unfortunately, there's very little help anyone can give you. The decision has to be yours and yours alone. You have to make it from your head and from your heart. Sometimes people stay when they should go or go when they should stay. If anybody tells you they can predict how it will turn out, don't believe them. Because there's always the story that proves you wrong.

Like this one: My ex-husband and I had a friendly dinner at the Plaza just before Christmas to discuss the kids. A couple at another table sent over a bottle of champagne. I had a glass—Donald doesn't drink—and we smiled our thanks at them. As they were leaving they stopped at our table and we chatted for a while. They told us they had been married for fifteen years with three beautiful children when they mutually decided that they wanted out of the marriage. They were divorced and each of them dated other people. But neither one married anyone else. And after nine years, they got back together and remarried. That was five years ago, and they appeared to simply adore each other.

The only hard and firm advice I can give you is to decide *something*. It's better to make a decision, even if it's the wrong one, than to live in a state of limbo, not here and not there.

But before you decide anything, be sure of your facts. Don't break up your marriage over a figment of your imagination.

About fifteen years ago my husband got in the habit of stopping off "with the boys" at a local cocktail lounge after work and not coming home till four or five in the morning. One night, unbeknownst to him, I called my baby-sitter, put on a wig and dark sunglasses, and followed him. To my surprise, he and his buddies were quite well behaved.

No flirting and no fooling around. From that night on I was no longer suspicious.

                                                              Lucille

Sonya was smart. Thank heavens she had sense enough to check out her suspicions before acting on them.

I personally don't see taking back a man who has been unfaithful. People are fond of telling you, Give it time, he'll get tired of her in a year.... But who's to say it won't happen again? Once the air is let out of the balloon, you can't get it back in, can you? Whether in private life or in business, it's almost impossible for me to continue with a person who has deceived me. As far as forgive and forget, well, let's just say I *never* forget. If someone does something bad to me, I might go on speaking to them, but I always have it in the back of my mind. I'm aware of it and very careful around them for years and years to come.

But other women tell me they have managed to overlook what happened and keep their marriage intact. Andrea, for example:

To those looking in, we were the fairy tale couple; above average financially, intensely in love, yet when I was thirty-six and my husband forty-three, he left us, and another woman was involved. Our two children and I were totally devastated! I hurt so bad that I thought at times I was dying. We were apart for five miserable months until he could see how empty what he was pursuing was. After he came back it was very hard at first, because all trust had been destroyed. But as I began to give him unconditional love and forgiveness, it began to nurture such healing, commitment, and unity between us. We had such desire for one another that we had not experienced before. Our children are so happy that we are a whole family. I like to use the illustration, the same sun that hardens the clay softens the wax. I could have hardened my heart and let our lives be scattered and broken, or let my heart be softened into forgiveness and understanding, resulting in the miracle of healing.

Andrea

Clearly, when it works, "forgive and forget" can be wonderful. But just as clearly, it doesn't always work, as Marcie's story shows:

It took me about three years to feel halfway human after my divorce. Just about that time, my ex-husband decided that he'd made a mistake and began begging me to let him come back. Like a fool, I did. So I was remarried and pregnant again when I realized that this time I was the one who made the mistake. He'd hurt me so much that the love I had for him had shriveled up and died. I stayed with him for another four years, trying to talk myself into feeling differently than I did, because I felt the children needed a father and an intact family. But I couldn't make my feelings go away, and what I felt for him now was closer to hate than love, with a lot of disgust thrown in. Finally, when my youngest was old enough for day care, I told him I was leaving. I took my kids and moved out . . . and I've never regretted it for a minute.

Marcie

During my marital difficulties, I got a lot of mail either urging me to "win" my ex-husband back or praying that he would return to me. Sometimes, when I read these letters I found it hard to understand *why* these women were so anxious to have their husbands back, given the marriages they described.

31

I believed, and still do, that the man is the spiritual head of his household. I submitted to him and his decisions for that reason. I loved him and was devoted to him, therefore denial of his adultery was very easy for me. I felt I was a good wife and we shared so much together that I just couldn't believe he would betray me as he did. He went far beyond just infidelity, he manipulated me to do what he wanted while he was already planning to leave me. My desire as always was to please him. My husband forced me (financially) to sign the affidavit of consent by not paying court-ordered support and filing on fabricated grounds. It would have cost me money I don't have to fight him. I am amazed at the lengths that man will go to get what he wants. He doesn't care if I eat or have shelter. I have never held a full-time job. I don't know if I could find one at this age—I'm forty-eight. It is frightening to have to support myself if the court doesn't grant me anything, and if they do, will he pay it? I tell you this to encourage you— you have great opportunity to win back your husband. I pray fervently that this happens to you.

Florence

Florence's husband sounds like a nightmare! I can't help but think she's better off without him, even *with* her problems. Problems can be solved, but a sadistic, selfish, heartless husband to be obeyed as "spiritual head of his household"? No way. Honey, you don't need this man. I hope someday you'll see that.

I would rather live alone than with someone this self-centered, selfish, and thoughtless.

Robin

In Robin's case, as in many others, the problem isn't infidelity but the fact that the couple simply isn't in love anymore. I think Robin's got the right idea. She feels he's self-centered and selfish and thoughtless—she goes off and makes a life without him. Of course every case is different, but I personally can't see spending your life in a dead marriage. My feeling is that you leave it all behind and go find somebody who makes your eyes sparkle and your nerves tingle.

And if you give up social position . . . well, social position won't keep your feet warm in bed. Look at Princess Diana. She traded love for social position. Maybe she didn't know that was the deal going in, but I doubt it. I'm sure someone explained to her early on that an intellectual and artistic bachelor in his thirties is not likely to have a lot in common with a teenager who lives to shop.

I don't think she believed them. She thought she could change him—or rather that her love would change him. It didn't work. You're not surprised, are you? But she was very young and it took her a while to figure out what the deal was: Marriage to this prince meant she would have high social position; everyone would admire her and curtsy to her, but she wouldn't have his love.

The truth is, she didn't have it so bad. Do you know how many women there are out there whose husbands don't love them *and* they don't have tiaras and palaces and people bowing and scraping to them? And don't forget those two beautiful, healthy boys! That's quite a blessing, don't you think?

The alternative would have been for her to walk away, get a divorce, and find a new man whom she adored. Ah, but she didn't want to leave all that luxury. . . .

Lately she seems to have accepted that her husband doesn't love her and shows no sign of ever loving her, and she's gone on to make a life of her own outside of the royal family. But she did do an awful lot of complaining and carrying on. Blaming her bulimia on him—some people believe it; some don't. Many say Diana wanted to

33

be a slim fashion plate, and if she was a little curvy the clothes wouldn't fit as well.

Now Fergie was a different story. Granted, getting caught sunbathing topless with a man who wasn't her husband had a lot to do with it, but still she had the guts to say, "I can probably have a better life than this." She gave up the tiaras and the palaces, took her children, and left. I don't blame her. However, she lived in a constant storm of criticism from the press, which was very unfair. They complained about the way she dressed; that's her taste, she has as much right to it as anybody else. They said she was fat; realistically, not every woman has a fabulous figure. Fergie happens to be a perfectly nice, lovely girl; I've met her several times. What ruined her life was getting caught. Okay, in the south of France all women sunbathe at least partially nude. But she can't. Number one, she's not French. Number two, she's a duchess, married to a prince.

I'm not a duchess, but being in the public eye, I know better than to take my clothes off anywhere but my bathroom. I don't feel safe even when I'm miles away from anywhere. I spent last summer cruising in the south of France on a yacht called the *Bella Rena*, a gorgeous 140-foot yacht I had leased. One evening we sailed into Cap Ferrat harbor. The view is incredibly beautiful, the little church with the cemetery around it, the boats, the fabulous villas—you *have* to come out on deck to look at it, and I guess the paparazzi know that it's a good time to strike, when all the boats come in for the night and the passengers are on deck.

But I'm never off guard. They "caught" me and my boyfriend Riccardo sipping champagne on the front deck of the yacht; it was cocktail hour, and my mother was with us. So the poor photographers had to make do with photos of Ivana wearing a modest bathing suit, sharing a glass of champagne with a man in the presence of her

34

mother. If Fergie had known what I know, she might still be in Kensington Palace.

Stay or go . . . it's not an easy decision to make. It takes a lot of agonizing. I've lived through this period with several of my friends—when *you* know but *he* doesn't know that you know, and you're pretty sure your marriage is on its way out.

It's a very tough time, and you know what they say: When the going gets tough, the tough go shopping. When we sense bad times, we women have a primeval instinct to provide for our family. It's some kind of female survival impulse. Probably the cavewoman stocked up on blubber or whatever they ate when her cave-husband gave her *agita*. Once we hauled out a club to go looking for small game. Today we whip out the credit cards and go shopping.

Elaine went grocery shopping: loads of canned goods, including dozens of cans of peanuts, coffee, jars of jam, you name it. She did this every time she caught her husband cheating. I don't think she'll need to buy any more detergent as long as she lives.

Victoria stocked up on shoes—fifty pairs in every basic color you can think of: black, beige, navy, brown, gray. I asked her if she didn't think they'd go out of style before she could possibly wear them all. She said, "Honey, a black pump is always in style."

Dierdre went out and purchased pantyhose. Hundreds of pairs of her favorite brand. Maybe I should get her together with Victoria.

Charlotte, whose husband gave the gown to "the other Mrs. X," bought herself a fabulous new car.

My friend Natalie* indulged in a top-to-toe overhaul. I got a call from her one day because she knew I was friendly with Dr. Stephen Hoefflin, a top plastic surgeon who practices in Los Angeles. Usually he's booked up twelve months in advance, but Natalie needed to get this done under deadline, if you get my drift, so she begged me to call Steve and see if he could fit her in. "Ivana," she told me, "I want to have an appointment *immediately*. I want that son of a bitch to pay for what my new man is going to enjoy."

Natalie had her face done, her nose done, her eyes done, her boobs done, her bottom tightened, liposuction, whatever you can imagine, she had it. She had been a sun worshiper and therefore had a lot of dark spots on her skin; every single last one was removed. I asked her how much it all cost, and she said, "I don't know, it has to be close to fifty thousand dollars—but that SOB is going to pay for it." She used a credit card, which was issued in both their names, so he had to pay.

If you are married to a man of means, and he is unfaithful or otherwise loathsome to you, I say, leave him, get yourself a great settlement—and before you do, take his wallet to the cleaners. Honestly, I'd have done it myself if I'd thought of it. A new car, stock the closets and the fridge . . . Oh well. Too late now. My own prebreakup shopping spree was much less impressive by comparison. I bought lots and lots of sheets for my children: Pratesi and Frette—very expensive, but they'll last forever. One thing I can assure you, my children won't have to buy a sheet for many years to come.

Why sheets? Who knows. But I bet if you ask around, your friends who've been divorced will tell you that they went on some kind of shopping spree just before the big blowup came. Perhaps they didn't spend as much as my friends did, but you can do plenty of damage in Caldor's when the mood strikes you—and the mood seems to strike with a vengeance when a marriage is breaking up.

It's just another form of self-protection, and of protecting the family, making sure that your loved ones don't go without. Sometimes a woman is so fearful of not having "enough"—companionship, emotional support, social support—that she stays in an unhappy marriage forever.

And sometimes she stays because of the children.

Many people will tell you that you should stay in an unhappy marriage for the sake of the children. Like Jessica:

> My small son was two when I divorced, and he was devastated. There has been no healing of those wounds in the more than forty years that have passed since then. Please consider your two healthy sons and beautiful daughter. Your husband will forgive you for the small annoyances which upset him and you will forgive him for whatever it is—small things, probably.
>
> Jessica

I don't agree. The things that separate couples are more than "small annoyances"—and if that child who was two at the time is still troubled by the divorce, I think there are probably other factors at work. I'm sure I'll get a lot of criticism for this, but I don't believe you should sacrifice your life for your children.

There's nothing wonderful about living in a tense, angry household. Living with hatred is demeaning and demoralizing. A friend of mine told me that she never saw her parents kiss—I mean, not a good-bye peck on the cheek. She never saw them hold hands walking down the street. I wonder if kids who never see affection between a man and a woman won't grow up to be very awkward with the opposite sex when it's time for them to have a boyfriend or girlfriend.

I'd rather the couple separate; he will always remain a father, she will always remain a mother, but they don't have to remain a couple and make every breath they draw a bitter one. The children grow up with a horror of what goes on behind their parents' bedroom door. And the worst thing is, they think it's normal. They think this is how married people live.

I do believe that it's much better for children if you go out and find somebody they can see you being sweet with. Also, I think you owe it to yourself to make the best life you can. I always say that life is not a dress rehearsal. You're here only once. Sure, you have to think about the kids—always. But I don't think it's necessary to sacrifice your own life in order to be a loving and responsible parent. I'd rather you find a way to make things work so both of you are happy. Mother Teresa is wonderful, but that's not who you and I are.

> Mom said she felt bad that the parents of a friend of mine were divorcing. I said, "They were always fighting. Maybe if they get a divorce they won't have to fight so much."
>
> Ivanka Trump

My daughter!

People—I think women especially—sometimes sacrifice themselves for their children in the hopes that they will one day give up their own lives to take care of their parents. If that's your case, I'm afraid you're going to be disappointed. It won't happen . . . and I don't believe it should happen. Your children will help you and protect you when you get old but will not give up their lives for you. Nor should they.

Each of us has our own life to live as best we can. I do suggest to women that they do things for the children, be as caring and loving as they can. But don't look upon them as the mainstay of your life. We have to build a life for ourselves, not count on other people to fill our time for us.

If your marriage is an empty shell and you're together only for the children, I say, go out and find someone else.

38

Let your husband do the same. Honestly, you'll both be better off, and don't you think the kids will be too, with two happy parents living apart rather than two enemies living together?

Children are by nature selfish. They have their own world: friends, school, hobbies. Today they grow up so fast! When they go on to university, you're going to hear even less from them. They'll call you, they won't stop caring about you. But sooner or later, they'll have girlfriends and boyfriends, and eventually, they will marry and start their own families. They'll live their own lives.

And you should too. The more fulfilling and interesting and challenging you can make your life, the more you'll enjoy visits and phone calls from the kids, because you won't be looking to get something from them that they can't give you. I personally don't feel that staying in an unfriendly or faithless marriage is fulfilling. And before you know it, the children will be out of the house and you'll be alone.

My eldest son, Donny, is away at boarding school much of the time, and though I still have two children at home, I'm a realistic person and I know that it won't be that way for long. Ivanka is thirteen and in a year or so, she's going to go to boarding school in Switzerland for a couple of years because I want her to get that certain European flair and learn languages, which to me are very important. The school she will be going to is in the French-speaking part of Switzerland between Geneva and Lausanne. Classes are held in English, but after school, everyone must speak French and she will pick up a smattering of other languages along the way, because the students are multinational. Then she'll come back to the States for high school and college. Even now, she has her life: school, after-school activities, and her friends. She won't want to hang around with Mama much longer. Not that she doesn't adore

39

me—she does. But she wants her own life too, and that's the way it should be.

Eric is eleven and in a few years *he'll* be going to boarding school. Donny has already been away for three years (he's seventeen). Of course Donny comes home for some weekends and all holidays, but he doesn't *live* at home anymore. Not in the same way that he used to. His focus is elsewhere. He's out of the nest.

Sometimes I find myself with a weekend when all my children are away. The house is so empty. And so quiet. Normally, there's yelling and crying and banging on the door and the dog yelps because they step on his tail—always some kind of commotion, the phones going non-stop, kids going in and out. I'm not a mama, I'm a dispatcher: play dates, karate lessons, piano lessons, doctors' appointments, constant trauma, fights. I have to come *right away* and punish this one, and the other one is crying, "She got me in trouble."

It's fun.

I remember Donny's first day at boarding school. He himself had asked to go away to school because at home, he always had to have security protection with him. He felt he could never be on his own. He wanted to be just another kid. At boarding school that's exactly what he is.

I drove with him to the school, we settled his things in his room, met all the people and walked around the campus, and then it was time to go. But I couldn't leave him just yet; I wanted a little more time with him. I asked if he wanted to go to dinner. He said, "Okay, Mom, but let's go to the next town."

I said, "Fine, but why?"

"Mom," he said, "if I walk into the restaurant with you, everybody will know that I'm Donald Trump, Jr."

I said, "So what? That's who you are."

"They'll treat me differently. I just want to be like everybody else."

I thought that was great. So we drove to the village next door, and I asked Donny where he wanted to eat. He said, Taco Bell. I'm not that big on Mexican food, but whatever he wanted. . . .

We went into the Taco Bell. They asked me what I wanted. Tacos, yes. That seemed to be the thing there. And a glass of chablis, please.

You can't imagine how they looked at me—like I had come from the moon. How should I know they don't serve white wine? I was never in a place like that in my life! Frankly, I still think they should get some; wine goes nicely with Mexican food.

When the bill came, I couldn't believe it. The driver, Donny, me, whatever friends he had along—we all ate, and it came to about fifteen dollars. You can't imagine the fuss when I tried to break a hundred-dollar bill. But that was all I had on me. Finally I found a twenty I had put aside for tolls and such on the trip back, and I used that to pay for dinner.

What can I tell you, I'm more a Le Cirque person than a Taco Bell person. But I love to share things with my kids, and I love to laugh with them, even if the joke is a little bit on me. I thought this story was funny—until the next day when I saw the paper. A *full page* of Ivana and Donald Trump, Jr., at Taco Bell, picture and story.

Poor Donny. So much for his desire to be "just another kid."

Sometimes a woman will have to try several times before she actually manages to leave an unhappy marriage. She'll go out on her own for a couple of months, then she gets lonely and insecure and goes back.

Alicia* left her husband about five times, and she says that each time was more difficult than the one before.

Alicia is gorgeous, intelligent, kind, funny, elegant, social. They had two wonderful sons together. What more could a man want in a woman? Apparently that wasn't enough for her husband. He began "fooling around" and eventually it led to his leaving her for his "new love."

Half a year later he asked to come home.

Alicia had been devastated when he left. When she had the chance to get him back, she grabbed it.

Which made her happy, right? Wrong!

Alicia told me, "Now when he said he was going to play golf on Sunday, I'd wonder . . . is he really going to play golf?

"I caught myself calling his office with some dumb question—'What would you like for dinner, darling?' Really, I was checking to see if he was where he said he would be. The trust was gone. I was never sure I could believe him."

Much as it hurt her, Alicia couldn't live with him anymore. She asked him to leave again. They've been divorced about twelve years, and he has married two more times and divorced both times. I know he'd come back in a second if she'd take him. Whenever I go to Alicia's house, he's there; he comes for a drink, he comes for a visit.

But she won't have him back.

Alicia was very important to me when I was going through my own divorce. At the time, I felt it was inconceivable that I'd ever love another man again, but she kept telling me: "You're wrong. You will."

She helped convince me that I would love again, and I'd like to try to pass that confidence on to you. I'm sure you didn't break up your marriage without good reason, so stick to it and don't go back.

People often tell me that they found marriage counseling or psychotherapy helpful when they were trying to

42

figure out what to do about their marriage. I got a lot of letters suggesting Donald and I see someone, or that I go for therapy myself. The truth is, I tried it once. I went to a marriage counselor, but I felt he let me down. I won't say any more about it, except that I'm not a big fan of therapy. But if it helps you, great. Go for it.

Some women tell me that it's better to have a female therapist. I go along with that. I believe that a woman is more likely to understand what you're going through and feel for you.

However, I'm a big believer in do-it-yourself. I think you can figure things out without outside help. Basically, you're trying to figure out if you want to spend the rest of your life with this person.

Ask yourself, How much do we have in common? You got married because you fell in love, but once the novelty wore off, maybe there's nothing you both like to do. In the beginning you want to please him so badly, you're willing to forgo doing the things you like in order to do the things he likes.

But as time goes on you start to think: Hey, I want to see this opera and if he doesn't want to go—too bad. And if I have to sit through one more disgusting boxing match with blood and sweat on my dress I'll scream.

He thinks: She doesn't want to play golf with me, I'll go with the boys.

Before you know it, you're leading entirely separate lives.

Now you have to figure out whether there's any point in trying to bring your paths back together, or if you've drifted too far apart to make it worthwhile or even possible. Here's a technique that you might find helpful. Take a piece of paper and divide it in two columns. In the first, put down all the things you love to do. In the second, put down his response to them.

For example:

I like to ski, he hates to ski.
I like to travel, he hates to travel.
I love opera, he hates opera.
I love being with the kids, he's just not a big family man.
I enjoy small intimate dinners, he loves big, noisy parties that give me a headache.

Then take another piece of paper and do the same for him. Put down the things he likes and the ways he likes to spend his time, and your response to them.

He loves golf, I hate it.
He loves boating, I get seasick.
His idea of a fun day is to go out fishing by himself; he enjoys solitude. I break out in hives if I'm in a place without a Saks.

When you look over your list, you might feel that the things that separate you are trivial and don't really affect your life together. Or you may just wonder why you're spending another hour with each other.

One way or the other, you'll know.

And then you can act on your knowledge.

Make sure you're certain of what you're doing, then make the move and stick to it. I don't see how you can plan for the future if you're always looking back over your shoulder, trying to second-guess yourself.

People do make mistakes, and there's always a tiny bit of doubt, but on the whole, I feel you have to be strong with yourself. My advice—and this is what I myself did— is to think it through very thoroughly, then once the decision is made, stop worrying about it and move on.

Wavering and wondering are big wastes of time, and living in the past doesn't get you anywhere. Done is done. Onward to bigger and better things is my motto.

*　　*　　*

If you decide you want a divorce, or are told by your husband that *he* wants a divorce—or even if you *both* want a divorce, things can get very complicated at this point. Of course, this doesn't always happen. If the divorce is going to be handled in a relatively civilized manner, perhaps he packs his bags and moves to a hotel. (I firmly believe that the wife should never leave. The marital home should be for her and the children.) But if one partner wants a divorce and the other doesn't want to give it, or if they both want a divorce but can't agree amicably on the terms, the couple can find themselves in a situation called Holy Deadlock.

You'd think that in a civilized world the legal system would not compel people to live together if they don't want to. But, in fact, until recently many states required proof of fault before granting a divorce. New York still does. It's not a consensual state. In other words, it's not enough to say that you can no longer bear to live with each other in order to dissolve your union; one of you has to prove that the other has done certain fairly specific things that the law considers grounds for divorce.

Very often, before the couple actually separates, one or the other, or perhaps both have seen a lawyer at least for an informal "what if" chat. And if so, chances are the lawyers have told both parties that no matter what happens they should not vacate the marital home. And the couple will start playing the terrible game of Who Leaves First.

Why is it so important that the other person move out first? It's not necessarily that the first one to move out loses. But the courts do tend to embrace the status quo, which literally means, "state in which," meaning the way the situation is now. If you're at home, you stay there. If he's not, he doesn't come back.

Attorney Ira Garr says, "Let's say the husband comes

45

to me and asks if he should move out. My gut reaction is no. If he moves out he's going to have to support the wife and family anyway, and he's also going to have to support a second lodging: a second rent, probably a second car, definitely a second refrigerator to fill. That's going to strain all but the largest pockets. And six months or a year later, when you're finally at the point of deciding custody, the judge sees that the children have been living with the wife. The initial reaction of the judge is going to be, 'Why should I change it? The kids are okay; they're in school, they don't have any tics, they're not having any problems. If I change their situation and cause trouble then it's my fault. I'd best leave things the way they are.' "

Also, the man often feels that if he moves out of the house, the wife has no incentive to come to terms with him. She's living in her own home, with her children—he'll never see the end of it. Why should she have to sign anything she doesn't like—especially something that might force her to move? She's like the army camped on the hilltop. She can stay there forever, repelling all invaders. It might be years before he gets her out, maybe never, especially if she's got the kids with her. Not that many judges will evict kids from their home for the sake of economic fairness.

So that's the man's point of view.

My point of view is different. As I said, I believe very strongly that the woman *should* always get the apartment or family home as well as the furniture and everything in it. And therefore it becomes obvious that she can't be the one who leaves first. So my advice is, no matter how anxious you are to be out of the marriage, don't be the one to vacate the family home.

You have to try to get him out.

Of course, he's trying to get you out.

Remember that Michael Douglas–Kathleen Turner movie of a few years back called *The War of the Roses?* That's the

46

best example of Who Leaves First. While they're each trying to get the other out, they turn the home into a lunatic battleground.

And so it becomes a war. Can he provoke her into leaving, or will she provoke him? This can be a very bad time: The marriage has died but the couple is forced to live together, each trying to make the other's life miserable enough so that they'll cry uncle and move out.

Raoul Felder says, "Given a situation where your husband doesn't want to give you a divorce, and he hasn't given you grounds to get a divorce in the state you're living in, sometimes a lawyer will suggest that you make living with you obnoxious. Start going out every night and don't come home until three in the morning.

"If that doesn't work, move your boyfriend in with you. Let your husband come home from work and find you giving dinner to the boyfriend. There's a point where somebody's self-respect will take over.

"One woman hired two very large bodyguards and brought them to live in the marital residence. Wherever the husband went, there they were: in the living room, watching TV; in the dining room, eating. The husband finally got fed up and called the police. The cops arrive, and the woman says: 'Let me introduce you to my guests.' There's nothing the police can do. The husband eventually couldn't take it anymore and had to move out.

"It's sad what one human being will do to another."

Raoul Felder claims that he's seen everything that was portrayed in *The War of the Roses* in his practice, "up to and including the destruction of each other's pets. I've had a wife put snakes in the marital bed to torture her husband. I've had another wife go to her husband's law firm and remove all her clothes and sit there naked, just to humiliate him.

"One husband I heard of used to carefully set out a pair of leather gloves and a rope on his nightstand each night. Wouldn't that drive you crazy? The tools of strangulation . . . He told the judge that the gloves were because his cat scratched him at night. Does that make sense to you? Not to me. But okay, let's say I accept that. Then what's the rope for?

"It seems that whatever the human mind can think up to torture another person has been done by husband to wife and wife to husband, up to and including murder. I've had a woman come into my office complaining bitterly about her husband.

"Next thing you know he was found shot four times, twice in the back. Allegedly she heard a burglar, whom she shot *back and front*. By the way, she was acquitted.

"Suicide attempts are almost routine. They're used to get sympathy, to convey threats, to get attention. Threatening suicide as a tactic isn't limited to one sex or the other. It's popular with both men and women."

Although more than one woman has been reduced to keeping a can of Mace at her bedside for fear of her husband, the harassment doesn't have to be physical. Merely going through daily life with an unfriendly human soul is torture. Nothing you do is right. He'll bitch and complain and make your life hell.

Maybe he'll be silent for an entire evening, and you heave a sigh of relief—and he'll start up just when you're going to bed. There goes your night's sleep.

Does he know that something he does annoys you? Clipping his toenails, eating in bed, flossing his teeth? You can be sure he'll do it often and with enthusiasm.

Guests are about to arrive. You chose a pink dress, he wants you to wear the blue. But you're already dressed! He says pink makes your face look puffy. So you put on the blue. Oh, but he didn't realize how tired blue makes you look.

Your hair is down, he thinks it makes you look old. Your hair is up, it makes you look severe.

You greet him at the door with a kiss, he tells you a smutty joke about why men can't sleep with their wives.

What he's trying to do is to undermine you so badly that you'll be ready to throw yourself off a balcony—or at the least get out of the apartment and leave it to him.

Don't let him get to you.

If it gets to be too much for you, have your mother or sister or a girlfriend stay with you and go sleep in the guest room with her. If you don't have a guest room, you may have to resort to the living room couch, but it might be worth it. If things get very ugly, you might need a third party there both as a witness and as a calming influence.

If all else fails, you can always wait until he goes to work, then call in a locksmith and have all the locks changed. But that's a pretty drastic step and if you're forced to take it, be prepared to have one very angry husband on your doorstep when he comes home and tries to put his key in the door. I think you should hire a security guard to be there if you have to go this route. If you can't afford to hire a guard, have someone—friend, neighbor, mother—be with you. No matter how furious he is, he won't break the door down or hurt you if there's someone standing there watching.

Your goal is to give him time to calm down. Try and convince him to move into a hotel or something.

Then, after he's had some time to get over his anger, and you can reason with him, you might say something like: "I don't want you to come home because I've decided that we have no life together. We can't go on like this, so we're going to end it now. It will be much better for both of us. Not just me. You'll have a better life too. You'll see. We'll still see each other. We have the children to think of. One day we may even be friends. But we can't live together anymore."

Use a soft, calm but firm voice. Whatever you do, don't

49

cry. Save the tears for later. Now it's of the utmost importance that you don't provoke his anger. But you do want to get your point across.

Men do awful things to women, but we women have been known to pull some doozies, too. For every story about what *he* did, there's a story about what *she* did. I managed to collect enough examples of bad behavior on both sides to make us all thoroughly ashamed.

There's the one where she cut the sleeves off all his shirts. Another lady gave all her soon-to-be-ex's clothes to charity before he had a chance to pick them up. I hope she remembered to take a charitable deduction on her tax returns.

Someone told me about a songwriter who had to get a court order to force his wife to return his record collection. She did . . . but every record was smashed.

And the one where he took a razor and sheared her fur coats down to the nub. (*"And,"* as Nikki exclaimed in horror, *"before sheared furs were even in fashion!"*)

There's the story of a friend of mine who was married to a well-known actor. California is a community-property state, which means that in a divorce everything is divided up fifty-fifty and each side gets half of what the couple owns. Now this actor had no intention of giving her half of what they had. There was a country house, which they had agreed he was going to get in the settlement. He turned as many of their investments as he could get his hands on into cash, took the cash, and attended wine auction after wine auction. He bought the most expensive wines you can get—hundreds of thousands of dollars' worth—and where did he store them? Of course. In the house that was going to him, with all its contents. He purposely did all this before their accounts were frozen by any legal action arising from the divorce, only my friend didn't put two and two together until it was too late. When the wife finally woke up, the money was gone and the wine was out of reach.

And then there's the husband who had a great art collection. His wife found out he was having an affair and she left him. She took nothing but her jewelry and a few of the smaller paintings. A little Monet. A Renoir. A Picasso or two. They were her insurance policy. And if he had a hard time seeing his way to giving her a proper settlement, she could always sell off a little piece of his beloved collection here and there. Eventually, I believe I heard, he got his pictures back, which tells me he must have given her her just due. They always say, great art can bring one peace of mind. . . .

Don't think that this craziness is limited to people of means. It cuts across all income levels. I heard about a woman whose husband had a middle-management job in an international company. Whenever the president came to New York, he stayed in a town house on the East Side that the company owned. Knowing that the president of the company was scheduled to arrive in New York for one of his periodic visits, this woman went to the company's town house, lay down on the doorstep with her baby, and refused to move. The staff went crazy, but the woman wouldn't budge. The limo bearing the head of the company pulled up. He stepped out . . . there she was. He didn't know her from a hole in the wall, but of course she explained it all to him. She told him in great detail what a terrible person her husband was. The company president was very sympathetic. He sent her and the baby home in his limo.

The next day he fired her husband. Well, why shouldn't he, now that she'd told him what a horrible human being the husband was. And I'm sure he didn't enjoy the embarrassment of the scene outside his town house after a trans-Atlantic flight. Who needs it?

But that woman I don't understand. Talk about killing the goose that lays the golden eggs. What's the point of losing the primary breadwinner in the family? How does that do the woman and her children any good? But sometimes people are too angry or too upset or too jealous to *think*. And then they do foolish things. Those who come out the best in divorces, I'm told, are the people who are able to think out strategy and make plans.

When I was researching this book one lawyer told me: "I always tell my women clients, 'Years from now all that will matter is the size of the check the client gets in the mail, not how hurt and angry she may have felt back then.' "

I don't agree with him. Your emotions and your feelings certainly do count. But you have to find a way to function without being blinded by them.

How do you do that?

By making a plan. Not necessarily a five-year plan or a seven-year plan. At this stage, it's enough to make a three-month plan. You are going to start gathering information.

In this game we call divorce, whoever has the most information wins.

When you eventually retain a lawyer to represent you in the divorce proceedings, he will go to your spouse's lawyer and request a financial statement. Your husband may not be so happy to supply it, but ultimately he will have to. But it's much easier if you already have all this information in your hands by then. That's why I think every married woman, even the most securely married on the face of the earth, should have complete information about her husband's finances. You're entitled to this information. There's absolutely no reason why you as the wife shouldn't know about every penny there is in the bank— where it comes from and where it goes.

But too many of us have no idea.

This search for the assets may not apply to a couple who make enough to get by and struggle like the dickens to put something away in a mutual fund. They probably know where every penny is. But in wealthier circles, very often the wife merely spends; she doesn't have any idea where what she's spending is coming from. She knows there's enough, but exactly how much is a mystery. Half the game is finding out how much he's got and where he's got it.

Raoul Felder says, "They say that the two people who really know a man are his wife and his valet. Well, I don't know about the valet, but the wife doesn't know beans about the man—and that goes for *all* income levels. The wife will tell me, 'My husband works in a bank.' I ask what does he do in the bank. She doesn't know. It's the same with the stock market or brokerage house or law firm. The wives know the name of the firm, but they don't know what the husband does there exactly.

"Looking at the statistics it seems as if a woman should start planning for the divorce the day after the ceremony—and a case could be made for the day before the wedding. How you go about this planning depends a lot on how long you've been married. If you've been married any length of time it becomes very difficult to interrogate your partner. You can't suddenly look up over breakfast after fifteen years and ask how his Eurobank investments are doing. The trick is to get him talking.

"Everybody talks too much. You'd be surprised how much a man will tell you if you approach him right, and if you can get him going."

This is information you are entitled to. It's yours. You are doing nothing unfair by getting it. Start immediately. Make photocopies of every paper that comes to the house with a dollar sign on it: bank statements *and* the canceled checks, brokerage statements, bills, all tax documents and tax returns—every financial document that comes to the house. Credit card statements *with* the charges.

Raoul Felder says, "If you get somebody's canceled checks and credit card slips, you can pretty much know everything about that person's life. You look through them and at first you'll get a sense of the music, not the words. Then you start to get a sense of the lyrics too. Soon your mind will start forming pictures, you'll get a sense of his lifestyle: his drinking habits, his eating habits, where he buys his clothes. A fairly detailed picture of this person evolves before your eyes. You might see dinner for one, dinner for one . . . suddenly, dinner for two. And a charge from a florist the day after the dinner. Now a charge from a chic women's store . . . more dinners. More flowers. More presents. Oops—a charge from Cartier . . .

"There's another way of getting to the truth of what a man has, a foolproof way. Most men of any substance have a little piece of paper hidden away somewhere on which they've written down exactly what they're worth. Down to the last penny. Trust me, they do. I've never seen one case where the man didn't have it. If I haven't seen it, it simply means I couldn't get it. There will be a little piece of paper somewhere on which, in the dark hours of the night, he's listed stocks, cash in bank, property. Everything. Down to the last little what-have-you. I don't know exactly why men do this, I just know they do. It reaffirms their masculinity or something.

"Do I have one? Everybody has one.

"Anyway, find that little paper and you'll find the truth. There are other times when men might lie and puff up what they're worth. But this paper will have the truth. When they're buying a house or a condominium, for example, they may have some worthless stock in a company, but they list the value as sixteen million dollars. Those 'little' lies can come back to haunt a man in a divorce case. He's all but *sworn* that he has this money, but he doesn't. You can torture him with that. Every divorce case has a weak spot. Everybody has something to hide. You've got to find it."

My friend Nikki: "You know what they say: You want to score, you've got to keep your eye on the ball. Every wife has to be a spy. Check everything. All phone bills. Receipts. Don't let anything go unchecked."

Raoul Felder has more suggestions: "Make a friend of your husband's secretary. If he has a secret bank account, ninety percent of the time she knows where it is. And by the way, it's almost always within ten minutes of the office. Men are lazy. Everybody needs somebody he can talk to without censoring, without thinking, just spouting off, and many men don't think of their secretaries as being real; they're nonpersons. So who better to let your hair down with than that sweet nonperson sitting across the desk? She knows all his secrets. Trust me.

"Even better is a *former* secretary. When he fires a secretary, *you* keep up a relationship with her. And if he was given to philandering, ex-girlfriends make wonderful tattletales. Gennifer Flowers is a perfect example. Men love to puff themselves up to their girlfriends. I'm not saying you have to keep up a relationship with your husband's ex-girlfriend just in case you ever wind up in a divorce court, but it wouldn't hurt to keep her current address stashed away somewhere. One thing I know, when you enter the wonderful world of divorce, nothing is too crazy, too far-fetched, too wild, to happen.

"How many times have I said, 'How do you know your husband doesn't have another family and another child?' 'Oh, don't be crazy,' they tell me. And yet it happens quite often. Men marry another woman, they have two wives and two families. Interestingly, women never set up two families. Only men do that."

It does seem to me that by knowing where your family's money comes from and where it's going, you can go a long way toward preventing deceit of any kind. He's got to pay for that second family somehow, don't you think? So not only will you educate yourself as to your family's finances but you might find out some interesting tidbits about your money and what your husband is doing with it.

Of course *you* won't lie, cheat, or steal, but spouses have been known to do so. If you have reason to suspect your husband is skimming his assets and taking them overseas to a Swiss bank or the like, I suggest you hire an investigator to look into it. If it turns out he's doing something illegal, your goal is not to get him into trouble. You don't want to put him in jail; you just want what belongs to you.

When you get this money, you declare it properly on your income taxes. What he does is his choice. But you might tell him what you're doing so he has the opportunity to do the same.

It's very important that you start keeping a daily diary. Write down where you went, who you saw together with your husband. If he said anything objectionable or abusive; if he hurt you or the kids. Write it down. It will tell you a lot—sometimes you won't even realize how much until a lawyer looks at it. Then it can become a valuable aid to testimony.

Apparently, the law says that if one person testifies that such and such took place on a certain day and the other person says it didn't happen, then it's a question of fact, which the judge has to decide. But if one person testifies that it happened on that date, and the other person doesn't remember, *then the first person carries the day.* Therefore a daily diary may become invaluable to you. There are three things a person can do, says Raoul Felder. "Keep records. Keep records. Keep records."

It will also help you to find out something you absolutely must know and can't really trust to memory: how much it costs to run your household; how much is spent on the children's education, vacations, mortgage and maintenance, insurance of all kinds (homeowner's, health, cars, boats if any), taxes of all kinds, staff if any, clothing, even gifts.

You're much better off gathering this information in the field, as it were, because later on, when you're asked to list them, it's so easy to forget small expenses that do mount up. I'll give you an example of an expense that you might easily forget, and that's birthday and hostess gifts for your kids. I'm glad Ivanka is popular, but sometimes I wonder if anybody has a birthday party in New York City without her. That's an item you'll have to include in your budget, and would probably never think of in the stress of the moment. If you catch these things now, you'll include them when you add up how much money you'll need for you and the children to live on.

If you own your house, you pay homeowner's insurance. How much is it? Is it a thousand dollars a year or ten thousand? What are the real estate taxes? What does the house cost you to run: gas, water, heat, electricity, perhaps repairs or maintenance or gardening costs, pool-cleaning service? You may not pay attention to these things until it's too late.

The destruction of a marriage—no matter who initiated it—is a difficult, heart-rending, traumatic experience. It's excruciatingly painful, especially if you're taken by surprise. Your world is rocked right down to its foundations.

You're devastated. You can't believe it's happening to you. You can't stop crying. You cry until there are no more tears left. Then you cry some more.

It hurts like hell. You burst into tears without warning. Some women become so depressed they need antidepressant drugs or even hospitalization, like Sarah:

I was taking the strongest mood-elevating pills four times a day and still couldn't sleep. I got down to eighty-five pounds. I would look for him in his car while I was driving. I went to places I thought he might be. I would call, crying; he would hang up on me. My heart wasn't just broken, it was in pieces. The killer was that I was being replaced by another woman. Everyone knew but me. Two weeks after our divorce, he married her. And I ended up in the hospital, due to exhaustion and nerves.

Sarah

I caught my husband with his twenty-two-year-old girl-friend. I'll be forty-one in September. It turns out he's been seeing her for a long time. Everyone else knew, all my friends and relatives. I was the last one to find out. I was so hurt. I felt like the whole world was mocking me, joking about me. I can just imagine how you feel, seeing yourself on the news every day. This was a very deep wound, and it's done by your own husband. I still feel hatred, anger, jealousy toward him.

Marilyn

Getting a divorce is probably not the worst thing that can happen to a person, but it ranks right up there as one of life's bigger tragedies. Please don't make the mistake of thinking that being wealthy makes you immune to the pain. No one is immune, whether you're rich or poor, famous or unknown.

I felt every horrible feeling these women did. I went through every lousy, miserable emotion. I wasn't spared a moment of suffering. Believe me, I know just what they're talking about.

Part 2

The Breakup

Chapter 3

The Explosion and
the Aftermath

I think by now everyone's heard more than they want to about the breakup of my marriage to Donald. I'm not going to discuss the intimate details—that's personal and, anyway, if you've been through it, you know what it's like.

I'm certainly not going to rehash the charges and counter-charges that were played out between me and my ex-husband. Thank God all that has been finally and amicably resolved, and this is the place for me to say that I wish Donald nothing but the best, and I know he feels the same way toward me. We have three beautiful children together, and I know their welfare is always uppermost in both our minds.

But, briefly, this is what happened—and all this information is in the public domain and was published by the press.

My family and I were on our annual post-Christmas ski vacation in Aspen, Colorado, in the last days of 1989, when I became aware that my husband was carrying on an extramarital affair. Donald, the children, and I were having lunch at a restaurant called Bonnie's, which is about halfway down Ajax Mountain; apparently, so was his mistress. Just as we were leaving, I became aware of her presence—I hadn't seen her before. The *New York Post* wrote: "Marla reportedly told Ivana: 'I love him and if you don't, why don't you let him go?' . . . Ivana . . . told the younger woman in no uncertain terms to stay away from her husband."

My husband left Aspen shortly after New Year's. I stayed on for the first week of January, as planned, and then flew home with the children. They had to get back to school.

> The other woman has everything to gain by stampeding the couple into public notice. It's unfortunate that you were humiliated on the ski slope. You have everything on your side: children, youth, health, wealth, right, dignity and brains. *Sit tight* and you can get him back if you want!
>
> Bernice

On February 11, my husband and I formally and legally separated. It was three days before Valentine's Day, a week before my birthday. I would be forty-one. The *New York Post* carried a picture of myself and my then-husband made to look as if it had been torn apart, with a one-word headline: SPLIT.

The article went on to say that "The storybook marriage of Donald and Ivana Trump lies in tatters. . . . The mega-developer became positively apoplectic over a newspaper item yesterday suggesting that Ivana was his business partner. That hit too close to home—and Trump decided to move out of their $30 million, 50-room triplex in Trump

Tower last night. His wife refused to talk to reporters. She said nothing. . . ."

Honestly, I think the press has nothing else to do when they interview the *pretzel seller* outside Trump Tower for his opinion on the breakup of my marriage. For the record, he said: "The Trumps' travails prove that certain universal truths apply equally to everyone. It's probably better for both of them." The *Post* went on to say: "Most people immediately assumed Donald was the villain and Ivana was the one who walked away, and said they didn't blame her."

That kind of talk is *not* helpful. Things are confused enough at that moment without seeing a daily commentary in the newspapers—and mostly lies.

According to the *Post*, another street vendor "speculated that Ivana is the one property on which Donald cannot engrave his name. 'He can't buy his wife with money. You can't buy love.' "

No, you can't buy love, but if you're very fortunate, it comes to you. I was one of the fortunate ones that week, because my friends and family chose to show me *at that particular time, when I needed it most,* how they felt about me. In that dismal week, the one bright spot was a girls-only birthday luncheon they threw for me on Valentine's Day (even though my birthday wasn't for four more days) at La Grenouille, one of New York's finest and most beautiful restaurants. Actually, the luncheon had been planned a long time before, but no one knew when they planned it what kind of unpleasantness I'd be living through when the day actually came, and that it would mean so much as a show of affection and support.

To my great surprise crowds of people lined the street— not just reporters and photographers but strangers, ordinary people who cheered me and shouted, "Ivana, we're with you!"

I was stunned. I could hardly speak; I just managed a

weak smile or two. But my heart was full of gratitude. When I got inside, they showed me to a private room where about thirty of my friends were waiting with the hostess of the luncheon.

My mother was there, of course. And so was Donald's mother, Mary Trump. His sisters came. My sister-in-law Blaine Trump came. I thought they were incredibly graceful to make that gesture and it was a wonderful show of support at a time when I really needed it.

Everyone said a few words, a toast about love and friendship. Many of them were funny . . . but I cried anyway. And I wasn't the only one. There were piles of gifts—all heart-shaped. That was the theme: love.

It was one of the most beautiful birthdays I ever had and one of the most meaningful. Who would think it, at a time like that? When we came out of the restaurant, we found that the crowd outside had gotten so huge that the police had to close Fifty-second Street—for my birthday party! Can you imagine?

We couldn't get through the crowd to my car. My friends formed a kind of wedge around me to protect me. People yelled, "Get the money!" and "Twenty-five million isn't enough!" I was incredibly touched by their humor, their love, and their support. All those people whom I had never met who took the time to come cheer me on my birthday . . . and all those who sent cards, letters, prayers. I got bagloads of mail—someone said it looked like the week before Christmas at the North Pole. The papers said I had become a "media goddess."

I think you are a person for all women to look up to and admire. A woman who can manage on her own and persevere under the most trying of times, a wonderful mother, and a person who never demeaned herself when everyone around her did.

Louise

I sure didn't feel like a media goddess. The truth is, at that point I would have given anything for the whole thing to go away. I still wanted my marriage and my husband, if there was any way that could possibly work out. The only public statement I made at that point was that I loved my husband. But I could not and would not tolerate what's known as an "open marriage," where one or both parties have affairs with other people. Honestly, I don't see the point of being married if you're going to have romances on the side.

I was twenty-eight when I married Donald, and in no hurry to marry at all. I was having a very good time in Canada. Donald wasn't famous in those early years. He was just a nice all-American kid, tall and smart, lots of energy: very bright, very good-looking.

He certainly wasn't fabulously wealthy. But I wasn't looking for fabulous wealth. I wanted someone I could build a home and a life with. If I'd wanted to marry for great wealth, I had plenty of chances. Donald was far from the wealthiest of my suitors. I married for love.

Nikki Haskell: "Ivana was so excited when they got engaged. I remember when she came to my office on Park Avenue to show me the ring Donald had given her. And, yes, it was there. You could almost see it with the naked eye. Okay, I'm exaggerating. But if some women get rocks, this was a pebble. It looked like a child's ring.

"Then she was married, and I kept saying, Ivana, you know it's time to get rid of that ring and get yourself something a little more . . . visible, shall we say? I mean, the ring is cute, it's nice. But it's *tiny!*

"She said, 'I will never not wear this ring.'

"You know what she told me? 'I don't need a big diamond ring. I only need this. The girls with the big diamond rings are the ones who've caught their husbands cheating on them. Those rings are payoffs. They weren't given in love.'

"And she wore that ticky-tacky ring as proudly as any person. We were out someplace one day and I saw El Rocko on somebody. I said, 'Ivana, that ring has your name on it. I want you to get a big ring like that. Enough with the toy jewelry. I'm embarrassed to be seen with you in public.' But she never took off that little peewee engagement ring she got from Donald. The first time she went out and got a really important necklace was for the opening of the Trump Tower. I mean, it takes the christening of a skyscraper to get her interested in some real jewelry."

I like jewelry but couldn't care less about stately pieces. I like to be comfortable. When you have "important jewelry," you have to worry about it. Who wants to spend their vacation waiting to get into or out of a safety deposit box?

But a big church wedding was something I had dreamed of from childhood. Donald's parents belonged to Marble Collegiate Church and that's how we came to be married there. We had a beautiful wedding . . . but it's not the same as the Catholic wedding with all the trimmings that I had fantasized about as a girl. I guess somehow I transferred the dream to Ivanka. I've always pictured her having a wedding in St. Patrick's Cathedral on Fifth Avenue. Ivanka was baptized in the Protestant church, but I go to a Catholic church and I take her with me. Both her nannies are religious Catholics and if I can't be there for some reason, they listen to her say her prayers at night. So you could say she's being raised in two religions, of both her parents.

One day Ivanka said to me, "Mama, if you want I'll be Catholic."

I said, "Never mind what I want, it's what *you* want."

"Mama, I would like to be Catholic and have a big wedding in St. Patrick's Cathedral!" said my daughter.

When, on February 15, the day after Valentine's, there was a headline trumpeting that my husband met his mistress when they sat in the same pew at Sunday services in the church where he and I had been married, I don't know why it should've hurt so much. But it did.

I couldn't believe the ferocity with which the press came after us. The week following our separation, *People* magazine had Donald and me on the cover, with the headline BILLION DOLLAR BLOWUP. *Time* and *Newsweek* ran big spreads on us, and newspapers all over the country were covering the story. (In Europe . . . don't ask. The story of our divorce ran in the *South China News*, for heaven's sake!)

Daily, there were newspaper articles speculating on our sex lives prior to and during our marriage. My children had to walk to school past newsstands where their father's picture was featured under a headline concerning adultery—and had to see references to their mother's "dark past." The *Post* claimed I had a "dark past," but they couldn't find anything to back that up, aside from my hair color. They built a whole story based on words like "nobody knows for sure." What nonsense!

The press knew no bounds—certainly not those of good taste. They speculated in print as to whether I had ever slept with my first husband. They said that I had hidden my first marriage. I didn't tell them about it because they didn't ask me. It's in plain sight on my marriage certificate that I had been married and divorced before. All they had to do was look. I don't lie—but there's no law that says I have to do their jobs for them.

A newspaper headline that quoted me as saying, "Gimme the Plaza, the jet and $150 million" was turned into *T-shirts* that sold for ten dollars! Do you think anybody actually wore them?

They made up lies about my "impoverished childhood," saying I was born in a "filth-ridden" apartment. That made me sick, it really did. I'm the neatest and cleanest person in the world! The *Daily News* claimed our story boosted its circulation by thirty thousand a day. The *Post* likewise—except for the infamous "Best Sex I Ever Had" headline, which they claimed boosted their circulation by *forty thousand*.

I was already in so much pain over the breakup of my marriage . . . crazed with worry over the future of my children; fearful about the ill effects they might suffer from all this; emotionally drained and confused and distressed. The press just made my life torture. The whole thing was sheer hell—hurtful and degrading—but there wasn't much I could do about it.

I kept my head high and rose above it.

I released a statement through my attorney: "This is an extremely difficult time for Mrs. Trump and her children. She is a family woman. Her marriage and her family have always been the most important things in her life. . . ."

> We women at McBride Co. in New Jersey would like to compliment you on your poise and character at this very difficult time. You have shown us a beautiful person in that you have never blemished your husband's name and have kept your feelings personal and tactful.
> Carmella, Frances, Eman

I made it a practice not to respond to the press reports, except on one or two occasions. For example, when they said I didn't have a master's degree, I arranged through my publicist for them to show my diploma on television. We tried to counter the untruth with the truth, the lie with the fact.

> This is a great-grandma writing to you. Please don't pay attention to all the trash in the news. You're a beautiful woman with a lovely family, so don't give up hope.
> Grandma Lil

Even during the worst of my ordeal, I never said a bad word about my ex-husband. Actually, I never said *any-thing* about him, good or bad. My only response was "No comment." I behaved with pride and dignity and I'm proud of myself for that. It's not easy, but you can do it.

And you can probably do it with some degree of privacy. I had to try to come to terms with what had happened to my marriage, attempt to work out an agreement with my husband, deal with lawyers, and most important, try to keep my kids from feeling *too* terrible—I had to do all that, under this constant media barrage, and keep myself from being derailed by it.

My children and I couldn't go out in the street without being mobbed by the press. Wherever we went, reporters shouted questions: Do you hate Donald? How do you feel about your father?

In order to go to work at the Plaza, which is across the street from Trump Tower, I would go down to the basement of Trump Tower, to the loading dock where arriving merchandise is checked in. My limousine would be waiting there, the windows and sun roof covered with wrapping paper—the tinted windows weren't protection enough from the flash cameras. The limousine would drive across the street and into the receiving room in the basement of the Plaza. From there I'd go up to my office, always by back corridors and elevators. I couldn't walk through the hotel or cross the public rooms.

I cried for myself, yes. But I cried bitter tears for my children. I can't tell you how bad I felt for the kids. They couldn't go *anywhere*, not to a restaurant, a movie, an ice-skating rink—nowhere. They had to be *indoors all the time:* either at school, at our home, or at somebody else's home. Eric, then only seven, found himself cut off from the playgrounds. Ivanka couldn't stroll in Central Park with her friends. Donny couldn't ride his bike. Photographers hung around outside Trump Tower lying in wait for them, following them if they ventured out.

If, by some miracle, the press let them walk to school in peace, there were the headlines screaming from every corner, seeming to vie with one another for the nastiest quote. There was no escape from it. My children had to see and hear about their parents' marriage breakup while simply going about their everyday business, and I felt awful about it.

Obviously, I stayed with the children as much as I could during this time, but at one point I had to take a business trip to the south of France to discuss the possibility of my endorsing a brand of champagne. As much as the children needed me, I also had to look to my future, our future. But I intended to make this trip as short as I could—just one day, so I would be away from them as little as possible.

I was sitting in the airport in Paris waiting for the connecting flight, when I got the call from my nanny. She said, "I don't know what to do! Donny is absolutely beside himself. He wants to call the *Post* and tell them that he has the best mother in the world—the nicest, kindest person in the world—and he wants them to stop saying things about her."

I told the nanny to tell Donny that I was on my way back home and to keep him from calling *anybody*. I turned around and caught the next flight home. Donny was absolutely wild. He said if he couldn't talk to the newspaper, he wanted to talk to the judge! "They can't say things like that about you—and Grandma and Grandpa, that you grew up in a filthy apartment."

I finally calmed him down. The last thing I wanted was for the kid to get into a shouting match with the newspaper. They would destroy him. But do I have great kids or what? I'll never forget the love I got from them at this time, especially Donny, the eldest, who seemed to feel so much for me.

Every time I turned on the television, there was something else about my family and my marital situation. It became unbearable. I saw that I had to get the kids away, and my parents too. (My mother had been with me when it happened. My father flew in from Czechoslovakia to join us when it all blew up.) None of us could draw a peaceful breath. So I took everyone to Mar-a-Lago, our home in Palm Beach, Florida.

In Mar-a-Lago, I didn't allow any television to be watched, and there were no newspapers. Generally when we went down there, each child would take along a friend or two; not this time. It was just our family—me, my kids, my parents. We shut ourselves up on that beautiful estate.

To say that my parents were upset by what was happening is a gross understatement. They were horrified. When I was growing up, we were a close family and we gave each other a lot of support and caring. My father was my best friend, up until his death. I'm very close to my mother to this day, but I had spent more time with my father. My mom wasn't athletic at all and my father was extremely so—a very good sportsman himself and later an international judge, so he had gone with me to my ski races from the time I was very young.

My mother refused to watch me ski downhill after one race when I hit the finish line with my nose. I was about ten meters away when I hit a big bump and felt my ski binding open up. I leaped into the finish line—literally. I slammed right into it, face first. My goggles broke and cut me. There was a lot of blood because facial wounds bleed profusely even when they're not that serious. It made a great mess. *My* wounds healed fairly quickly, but my mother's didn't.

I credit my ability to weather some of the storms I've

been through to my sports background, and above all to my parents' love, teaching, and support. I've had lots of sunshine in my life. I consider myself a very lucky person. But this time I'm telling you about, when my marriage crumbled around me, was a very dark period. And I know that my background helped me get through it.

One of the misconceptions people have is that my life was a Cinderella story, where a girl with nothing marries the prince. Not true—and I've never liked that story much anyway. I've always thought Cinderella should have said good-bye to those nasty relatives, cleaned herself up, gotten a nice job and a cute apartment somewhere. Then she wouldn't have to worry about fitting into a glass slipper; she could buy all the shoes she wanted, glass, leather, suede, whatever, and meet the prince on an equal footing. (Ouch! Sorry.) In any case, when you've got a couple of bucks in your pocket you can hail a cab when your coach turns into a pumpkin. And, anyway, marketable skills are more dependable than fairy godmothers.

The other misconception people have is that I was always so wealthy I have no idea what real life is like. Nothing could be further from the truth. I'm not out dancing every night the way some people think. My life most of the time consists of kids, work, work, work, kids, time with my friends, dinner, and bed. When I go out, I'm very visible, and it may be reported in more than one newspaper, so people get the idea that I flit from one elegant ball to the next.

The truth about my upbringing is somewhere in between. We weren't rich and we weren't poor.

I grew up solidly middle class. In Czechoslovakia when I lived there (things are obviously changing now) there was no such thing as poor or wealthy. Everyone was middle class. Everybody had about the same amount. There was no incentive for people to kill themselves at work because you could go so far and no further. Whether you worked eight hours a day or sixteen, you still got the same salary. So people would go to work at 6 A.M. and leave at 2 P.M. The afternoon was free for sports, movies, whatever. By two o'clock Friday afternoon, the cities would be deserted. Almost everybody had a little dacha (a country cottage), which they most likely built themselves. It might be nothing more than a small cottage on a tiny parcel of land, but it was a place to escape to, to see their friends, play sports, and generally enjoy life. Why not? There was nothing else to do.

In America, as soon as people get a little taste of success, they start to work even harder. They want more money, which leads to longer hours, which leads to more money. But how many steaks can you eat at once? How many cars can you drive?

I'm not knocking the free enterprise system, but it can be a trap. Couples can be so busy "making it" that they forget to "make it" with each other. They have no time to talk, to communicate, which is the most essential part of any relationship.

As a young girl I had no idea that someone could buy a bigger car than the next person, or a better home. Or that by working hard and developing your talents, you could advance more than someone else.

When I was about twelve, I went to Austria for my training for ski races. Until then my only experience of foreign travel was when my parents would drive me in our car for vacations to the Baltic Sea in Poland, or to Romania and Bulgaria. I saw the poverty there and I was glad I lived in Czechoslovakia. I could see the difference and was very grateful for what I had.

But now, in Vienna, this was the first time I saw the world on the other side of the Iron Curtain—and I couldn't believe my eyes. The vegetable market! The meat market! The (to me) exotic foods available to anyone! And so many different kinds! It was February and they had strawberries for sale. You could just go up and buy them . . . if you had the money. And you could get the money by working harder than the next person and excelling. . . .

The wheels were starting to turn in my mind.

I don't want you to get the idea that we were lacking in Czechoslovakia. We had plenty of food, but it was what we or our neighbors grew or raised ourselves. We were never hungry, but we did not have strawberries in February. Oranges and bananas, for example, didn't grow locally and were unknown, at least to me, when I was a child. I think my father bought me my first bananas—they came from Cuba, I remember—for Christmas one year. The country had no money to spend overseas on luxuries like oranges when they needed rubber and other industrial products, but somehow bananas were put up for sale that one year. My father stood in line for two hours and managed to come home with three or four bananas—there was a limit, so many per customer. I tasted this new food—and I hated it. My poor father was so disappointed.

As a result of my upbringing, in my home even today we don't waste food. I can afford any food in the world, I could throw it out the window if I liked—the cost is not the point. I don't like wasting food. Not that I'm one who takes a doggie bag out of the restaurant when there's one shrimp left on the plate. But I do teach my kids to take only as much as they can eat. They can always have another portion.

On the weekend, at our home in Greenwich, there are usually lots of people and lots of food. Then on Sunday evening or Monday we finish what we have. I don't throw things out. Often we make a huge turkey. It makes a wonderful meal and great leftovers for the kids and their friends to pick at. We eat that, then kids eat enormous turkey sandwiches, which they love. And *then* out of the bones, you make a soup with rice and it's delicious. I got the recipe from my ex–mother-in-law, Mary Trump.

That's one of the many lessons I learned from my childhood: to enjoy food but not to waste it. When I was a girl, food was plentiful and delicious, and it was all grown or raised right there. We had almost every kind of meat with the exception of veal. Veal was a real luxury because they wouldn't kill the calf, they'd wait for it to grow up and have a whole steer. But you could get any kind of beef, chicken, ducks, pheasants, turkeys. As all Europeans do, we'd eat all the insides and outsides: sweetbreads, kidneys, liver, and we even pickled the pigs' feet.

Each year my grandmother raised a pig, and in the beginning of January, we'd call the butcher, who would come and slaughter it. I was always beside myself. They waited for the cold months, because the meat would last longer. We would make sausages—bloodwurst, whitewurst, strong sausages, head cheese. They would smoke the meat, pickle the feet. We'd have food for months out of the one pig. All this was done in my home. Today it's all done in factories.

At Easter, we'd have baby lamb, which was gorgeous. We had all kinds of cheeses, sheep's milk, cow's milk. There was fish from the lake—it couldn't be fresher. Fruits were eaten in season—strawberries, blueberries, every kind of berry there is. In winter we'd eat preserved fruits. Carrots, celery, onions, and potatoes we could store as they were, and apples keep very well in a cool place, but other fruit we'd can, whole big peaches the way they do in Europe in those enormous glass jars with the rubber tops. My mother would put up jams—cranberry, raspberry, blueberry, gooseberry, the most magnificent jams you can imagine, shelves of it lined our cellar. Grapes they would hang on strings in the air and they'd hold until early March.

Our town, Zlin, was a factory town like many others.

A large shoe factory was the main industry and the main employer. But there was one unusual thing about the town: Up in the hills there were movie studios, and from the age of four, I was chosen to be in them. I did about eight films as a child. I wonder where that footage is today.

I didn't think I was special. It just happened. I had very long hair and I guess it made me stand out. When my parents would take me on the tram to visit my grandparents, strangers were always pulling at me, grabbing me, wanting to touch my long curls. They'd literally take me from my father's hands to play with me.

In then-Communist Czechoslovakia, you got the best schooling available for free, just by going to public school. The best medical care—for free. All my sports training, equipment, everything was paid for. Czechoslovakia gave me a beautiful childhood, a very safe childhood, with no alcohol, no drugs, no discotheques—but a lot of culture and a wonderful education. The Czechs are a straight-forward people with great values.

The problem is that you can go so far and no further. They build you up, with training and education—they urge you to take a master's degree—then they stop you cold. You cannot excel. They wanted you in line, not to stand out, to be just the same as everyone else even *with* your education and training. So nobody breaks their neck at work, since they can't achieve too much.

But that little view of the outside world—that trip to Austria when I was twelve—planted a seed in me. I knew something I hadn't known before: that it was possible to achieve, to stand out, to make something of yourself beyond what you started with. That was the moment I said to myself, there's no way I'm spending the rest of my life in Czechoslovakia.

My grades showed me I was smart. I had guts. I wasn't afraid to work. I knew I could make it.

And that, too, I owe to my father. He was a swimming champion. I was born prematurely, at seven months, and I was a puny little weakling; they kept me in an incubator for two months. My father said, "I'm going to make this little baby strong." At the age of two, my father dumped me into a pool and taught me how to swim.

At four, he put me on skis and I loved it. By six I was winning my category in races, both swimming and skiing. Between six and twelve I won most of the races in my category in both swimming and skiing.

Twelve was the cutoff age when training became very intense because at that point you're in sight of the Olympic team and all your efforts are focused on making the team.

I was a contender in two sports, skiing and swimming.

Swimming is an upper body sport; you pull yourself along with your arms, and the legs are secondary. Skiing is just the opposite, all legs and tummy, and the arms are just for balance. But I was strong overall, and since swimming championship competitions were in summer and skiing was in the winter, I managed to do both until the age of twelve. At that point my parents got together with my coaches and they agreed that I had to specialize. "You can't be the world champion in skiing *and* world champion in swimming," they told me. "It can't be done. You have to choose."

My parents left the decision up to me. That was the way they were. They had great faith in my judgment and were willing to stand behind any choice I made.

The weekend after my parents spoke to me, by chance there was a swim race scheduled in town and a ski race in the mountains. My parents left me with my grandma and told me, Wherever you show up, that will be what you've decided. If you go to your swimming race, that's the sport you chose. If you show up in the mountains, you're a skier.

I showed up in the mountains. By the age of fourteen I was on the women's ski team, having bypassed the junior division.

When I immigrated to Canada, I found myself with a bit of a problem. In Czechoslovakia, I was very successful. I had tons of friends and contacts. In Canada I was just a not-bad-looking girl who could ski. Nobody knew me. And although I spoke Czech, Russian, and German fluently, Yugoslavian and Polish quite well, I quickly found that the average Canadian man-or-woman-in-the-street is a bit weak on the Slavic languages.

New country. Almost no friends. No contacts. Don't speak the language. What did I do?

I didn't panic.

I didn't quit.

I didn't even go home to Mama.

I went to Berlitz.

People always seem to tease me about my accent and the funny way I say things. I've been known to speak of bolts and nuts. Would you tell me what's wrong with that? And if I've slept well, I say, 'I slept like a wood.' But so what. Everybody understands me. I never had any problem communicating.

I can't dance and I can't sing and I can't act in the professional sense, but I have certain strengths and I know I can rely on them. That's one of the reasons I survived my divorce as well as I did. I tell you openly, there were many times I was scared to death . . . but underneath it all, even in my most troubled times, I never lost my belief in myself. I knew that I'm willing to work hard—in fact, I like to work.

I owe my parents a great deal. They had a lot of confidence in me, which is probably why I have a lot of confidence in myself. But that doesn't mean that during the time my marriage was falling apart I didn't have many, many moments of pure despair. Real anguish.

I felt abandoned.

I was no longer part of a couple.

I was very scared. Absolutely terrified. I was more frightened than I could remember being in a long time. The world was one big unknown, a giant question mark. What would happen to me? Would I be able to cope? Where would I go? What would happen to my children? Would I have to move out of the apartment?

Most frightening to me was this sense of being power-less, seeing all the neat plans I had made for our future undone. As I've said many times, I'm a great planner and organizer. You have to be to run several homes, raise three children, have an active social and charity life and, last but not least, a demanding work schedule. My security lies in my calendar. I can leaf through it and see where each of the children will be on weekends for the next few months; whether with me, or their father, or a friend. But during that bad time when my marriage broke up, I didn't even know what the next morning would bring, let alone the next month.

I felt a tremendous sense of failure. I worked very hard during the fourteen years of my marriage. I tried my best in everything: making homes for our family; raising our children; being a good daughter and daughter-in-law; working in our business ventures.

I did my best, and it was *not* good enough.

My actual forty-first birthday was February 20, and I spent it with my children and my parents in Mar-a-Lago. Donald flew down to Palm Beach that weekend, and we had a small party, just the family. His parents were there too, and they were very distressed about everything that was going on, the breakup of our marriage and the horrible publicity.

79

I still had to work; I had a job, responsibilities, so I left everyone safely tucked away in Palm Beach and flew back to New York to take care of some business. I had to sneak into the Plaza through the private staff entrance so as not to disrupt the whole hotel. And there I found my office filled with pink and white balloons. There was a Happy Birthday sign, and flowers everywhere.

The staff of the Plaza had arranged yet another birthday party for me. About eighty people gathered in the Versailles Room to sing "Happy Birthday." The cake was chocolate amaretto and mousse, three tiers, and it said "Happy Birthday, Ivana. We love you." There was a lone candle in the center.

I blew it out with tears in my eyes . . . how could anybody not be touched? I had to respond to all this, so I said, "By now everybody knows every aspect of my private life. I'd just like to thank you for your thoughtfulness. Some of you have been working here for fifty years. I am really looking forward to being here with you for the next hundred years. I'm never going to let you down, and I know you're never going to let me down." I raised my glass: "To happiness and to love and to all of us."

I don't know how I would have survived without the encouragement and support of my family and friends. I hope that you, too, in this difficult time, have people in your life you can rely on.

People often think my divorce from Donald was the worst thing that ever happened to me, but as I've said, it wasn't. Divorce is painful, but you're alive, he's alive. You're not in love with the person anymore, but life still goes on, and there is still the hope that you might get together again, if you need to cling to that idea in order to help yourself cope. It allows you to get used to the idea of a life without your man gradually, to ease into it. And even if you never become lovers again, as long as you're both alive, there is at least the chance, however slim, that once the bitterness passes you'll be friends. But death is final, and especially when it's sudden, as it usually is in a young person, it's very hard to bear—far more difficult than the breakup of a marriage.

When I was very young, I loved a man and he was killed in a car crash. When my fiancé was killed I remained in a kind of near-coma for several weeks. I slept constantly and just woke up for a short time. It wasn't physical. I believe it was some kind of denial mechanism that allowed me to keep the terrible truth out of my mind. It took me a long time to really grasp what had happened. For about five years afterward, I couldn't manage to talk about it without bursting into tears.

George was a lyricist—a poet, actually—who set his words to music his brother wrote. As a youngster, I always wrote short stories and poems, so I admired George's incredible talent. It was amazing living so closely with an artist. You'd go for a walk in the woods or something and the next day it was part of a song. George was the best-known lyricist in Eastern Europe—the only man I ever went with who was already famous when we met. George was very facile, very gifted. He'd hear the music once through and he'd have the words ready.

But he also lived a very bohemian life. And he drank.

When it happened, we had both just come back from a short trip to Munich. I had been shopping for clothes for an upcoming modeling job. George had been on a concert tour of German-speaking countries with his band. I had things to do, so he went to lunch with friends and we arranged that he would pick me up in the evening and we'd drive to our country house together. But he forgot something at the country house and figured he'd make a quick trip there by himself to get it.

It's pretty much a sure bet that he drank wine with his lunch and perhaps his reactions were a little bit slow. I don't know and it wouldn't really have mattered. He couldn't have avoided the crash. As he drove through the woods, a huge tractor shot out from somewhere and plowed into him, sending George's Porsche into the air like a feather. George was thrown from the car.

He was killed. The other guy didn't even go to jail because there was alcohol in George's blood.

I was twenty-two. George and I had wanted to get married and now it seemed that I was widowed before I ever had a wedding. His death had a lot to do with my leaving Prague and going to Montreal. I wanted to get away from the city, the friends, the restaurants, which all reminded me of George. I knew it would be impossible for me to go on with my life there without George.

I do think that in the early days after your marriage breaks up, you should think of yourself as a mourner, someone who has suffered a loss. After all, it is a death, the death of your marriage, your partnership, your young dreams.

And a loss of innocence. When your marriage breaks up, you lose a kind of trust and I don't think you ever quite regain it; not in the same way. To this day I don't trust many people. Just two or three perhaps. Yet there's no real reason why I shouldn't be trusting. People are very nice to me. But when my marriage to Donald broke up, something in me . . . I don't want to say "died," but it changed. I don't know if I will ever be as trusting as I once was. I don't think I'll ever let my guard down as totally as I did. You can understand that. I just don't want to get hurt again.

Your old self-image, the way you thought of yourself, is gone forever, and you will have to rebuild your self-confidence practically from the ground up. Now you doubt everything about yourself—your appeal, your talents, your sexuality, your parenting ability. Your self-esteem is very low indeed.

In particular, your confidence as a woman is shattered. The deepest part of your femininity has been severely wounded.

Allow yourself to mourn. It's appropriate.

Only someone who has gone through it understands. The pain and humiliation are unbearable.

Lisa

In the first few weeks, I believe you should cry as much as you want, scream, let it out. Get all those feelings out of yourself. Some people try to hold it in, but all you're doing is postponing it. It will come out years later in a much worse way.

After a while the grief, the sadness, the humiliation, the fear, and despair all turn into a powerful, nearly combustible, all-consuming sense of rage.

And that rage brings with it an overpowering desire for revenge. You feel like you could tear your partner limb from limb. The urge to "get the SOB" is almost irresistible.

He ruined your life.

You're going to ruin his.

Wait till he sees how miserable you're going to make him. He's going to be sorry he ever did this.

This is when people hire barracuda lawyers and tell them to "get him."

This is when couples start to talk badly about each other, when they dump as much dirt as they can on their ex-partner. There couldn't be a better example of this than Woody Allen and Mia Farrow, who aired the most disgusting charges and countercharges in the public press. I remember being so embarrassed for my children's sakes. They read newspapers. What are they supposed to think, that people are animals? How do you explain two so-called loving parents tearing at their children like hyenas at a carcass? How do I explain to Ivanka that disgusting charge about the father molesting his child? I feel it's damaging to my children just to read about it; can you imagine what it does to *their* children? I feel sorry for those kids.

How you handle this stage is critical to the outcome. I can't stress that enough; but I do want you to understand that each of these stages is part of the process—a healthy, normal part of the process. You have to get through these stages in order to come out the other end. It's very much like the process people go through when a loved one dies.

You can think of this as an illness of the soul, with definite stages, just like a physical disease. And when you're sick, you may have your husband and children or your family with you twenty-four hours a day if need be, to help you, to comfort you, but it's still *your* illness. You have to conquer it by yourself. The battle is between you and your cancer, or whatever. This is the same. Divorce is something you have to face alone and recover from alone. Others can be by your side, but no one can do the job for you.

I know what I'm talking about. During the crisis period of my marriage, I lost about eighteen pounds. I weighed about a hundred and three pounds on my five-foot, eight-inch body. I was a bone!

But I had three children who needed me and I wasn't going to let my life be run by a situation I found thoroughly unpleasant. I always felt I could do better for myself.

It may take a while, but there will come a point where you've cried and screamed and cried some more and eventually you calm down.

You become able to function again.

You can take a more realistic approach, rather than feeling like you're in the middle of your worst nightmare.

It begins to dawn on you that although something terrible has happened, you're still alive. Your kids are okay, or they're going to *be* okay.

You're all going to come through this. Life didn't end on the day your marriage did.

Finally, you're going to get a glimpse of the idea that there *is* a future for you. You're going to be able to plan.

You may not think so now, but you will. I'm going to help you.

As upset as you are, you're going to have to pull yourself together. Some of the decisions and the choices you make during this period will affect the rest of your life, and probably none of them as much as the divorce lawyer you hire. It's absolutely critical that you find yourself a good lawyer, so much so that I've devoted an entire chapter to helping you do it.

Chapter 4

Lawyers and Legal Matters

I've had good lawyers, bad lawyers, and incredibly awful lawyers who didn't seem able to accomplish the simplest thing. Good, bad, or awful, one thing they had in common, they were all very, very expensive.

The good lawyers at least do a job for you. The bad ones, as far as I'm concerned, rank right up there on the scale of selfish cruelty with vultures, paparazzi, and some tabloids. I believe that women are being done in twice, once by their ex-husbands and once by their own lawyers.

I always knew I'd call all kinds of trouble down on my head if I told you what I really think about lawyers. That wasn't going to stop me—but lo and behold, *The New York Times* did it for me. On the morning of Wednesday, May 5, 1993, I opened the paper to read about the report issued by a panel appointed by New York State's highest court to investigate abuses by divorce lawyers. The report sharply criticized some lawyers, saying that they pressured women at a terribly vulnerable time in their lives; they'd tell them little about the progress of their cases, and then over-charge them to boot.

I could have told them that and saved them the nine-month study.

The report went on to say that lawyers often stretched out cases (and therefore fees) by filing motion after motion. In some cases, lawyers waited until crucial points in the proceedings to demand payment from women; they demanded assets or mortgages on assets up to and including the house the woman was living in! If the woman refused, they'd threaten not to try the case. The panel commission concluded that women need to be given greater protection from their divorce lawyers.

Why didn't they just ask Ivana?

I do not know how much the opinion of a seventeen-year-old girl means to you, but I felt very strongly that I had to write you. My father is going through some kind of life change. He gave up a very beautiful wife and has done very awful things, all for a voluptuous teenager. I want to say to you what I say to my mother: Don't you ever give up—fight until you get what you deserve. Most of all, do not ever dare feel inadequate because of what has happened. I wish you the best of happiness and luck.

Whitney

Whitney, you are one smart seventeen-year-old—and yes, your opinion does count with me—very much so.

When my marriage broke up, I didn't have a lawyer of my own. Donald and I had many attorneys for our various businesses, but that was the problem: They were lawyers for both of us.

I needed somebody of my own.

Even before Donald and I separated, I made an appointment with a friend, the well-known lawyer Raoul Felder. I told him what my prenuptial agreement said, what I thought was happening in my marriage, and asked his advice on what I should do now. All told, I spent about two hours with him. I didn't use him as my divorce lawyer, I merely paid for a consultation. He gave me a legal "take" on my situation and explored several different "what ifs" with me.

Being well known is fantastic for making restaurant reservations, but it's not so great when you're trying to accomplish something without the entire world knowing. In these large Manhattan office buildings, the elevator man, the doorman, the candy vendor, and the secretaries often have contacts in the press. They phone in a tip and they get a little something for their trouble.

Poor Jack Nicholson was "spotted" in the waiting room of a noted hair replacement surgeon and it wound up in *People* magazine. I got caught when all I was doing was trying to figure out what to do with the rest of my life. A day or so after my meeting with Raoul Felder, a newspaper wrote that Mrs. Ivana Trump was seen crossing the lobby of the office building where Raoul Felder has his offices. Could she have been seeing the famed divorce lawyer?

Maybe it wasn't the staff. Perhaps I just had the bad luck to cross the lobby at the same time as a reporter. In any case, I wasn't ready to have my plans made public. I hadn't even *made* plans yet. All I had wanted was some information: If I did decide to get a divorce, what would the next couple of years be like for me and my children? I wanted to know what we'd be facing.

I certainly didn't want the press to push me into a decision I wasn't ready to make. On the other hand, I didn't want to tell an out-and-out lie either. But luck handed me a way out. The paper said "Ivana" was wearing a brown suit. My phone started ringing off the hook with reporters asking me for a comment.

I told one and all—truthfully—that I have never owned a brown suit in my life. I like brown on other people, but

The Breakup

I don't feel it does anything for me. I told them they could look in my closets if they wished, and if they found anything brown then I would plead guilty. But clearly, the "woman in the brown suit" couldn't have been me.

You'll notice I didn't even touch the question of whether I had been to see Raoul Felder wearing something *other* than a brown suit. They were so fixated on that point they forgot to ask, and I didn't remind them.

Maybe I should have had the lawyer come to me? No, my doorman would recognize his name.

Okay, I'll meet him at a friend's house. Oh, but my friend might find the urge to spill the beans too much to resist.

Perhaps it's best to meet at a café? But then if we're spotted they'll say I'm having a romance with the lawyer!

Sometimes there's just no good way out.

My ex-husband, to whom I was married for twelve years, was a person of influence in Chicago. Because of his connections, money, and my dishonest attorney, I lost everything. The biggest lesson I learned is that a very honest attorney who has only your interests at heart is a must.

Esther

After twenty-seven years of marriage and being a homemaker, housekeeper and raising five children, my ex left me for a younger woman. I got screwed with my divorce since whatever I did as a homemaker went by unnoticed without a substantial monetary gain. I was also unfortunate in getting an unsophisticated attorney, who I felt was "strictly for the men," the type that likes to keep women down.

Jeanne

I didn't print these letters to frighten you. But I don't want you to be one of many women who learn too late how important it is that you find an honest, resourceful, capable lawyer who is willing to fight for your rights.

Of course, I'm talking about a situation in which there is something to divide beyond the books and the dishes. Often when people of means marry, they sign what is called a prenuptial agreement, known familiarly as a "prenup." A good prenup will spell out in a fair way what you will receive in the event of a divorce, taking into consideration such matters as how long the marriage lasted, and whether there were children, and how many.

Many women are afraid of prenuptial agreements. They feel they're too businesslike. After all, marriage is an affair of the heart. You're madly in love, floating on air, how could you possibly deal with something as down-to-earth as *money?* And the possibility of divorce? Why, there's no chance it will happen to you. No way. You two love each other. Accountants, lawyers, net worth—it's so unromantic. And what do we need it for, anyway? This marriage will be forever.

If so . . . God bless you.

If not . . . listen to Nikki.

Nikki Haskell befriended me when I first moved to New York. She was one of the first people I met, and she taught me all about the place. As she herself is the first to say, she's smarter than most of her friends—and for sure a lot funnier.

Nikki says, "I'm of the school that believes that you get more going in than you do coming out. He's never going to feel kinder and more generous toward you than he does at the beginning of the marriage. When you're breaking up it's too late. The trouble is, if he suggests having a prenup, the woman often thinks he's afraid of her taking all his money, when in reality he's going to give you more now than he ever will later."

Nikki freely admits she wishes she'd used some of these smarts in her own life. She's been married twice—to the same man. As she says, "Two marriages, one groom, two mistakes. The second time we married, he wanted me to sign a prenuptial. I was outraged. I wish I hadn't been so outraged. If I had one, I might've been protected a tiny bit. As it is, he wound up taking me to the cleaners—twice.

"Anyway, there's no harm done by having it spelled out in writing before the wedding ceremony. Think of it this way. If the marriage works out, he'll be giving you whatever you want anyway. And if it doesn't . . . you're spared all that screaming and hollering.

"As far as I'm concerned, the only time you don't need a prenuptial is if you marry a man who has no children and he looks like he's going to kick the bucket in about six months. He's got a bad cough and a walker."

Nikki tells this story: "I had a girlfriend who was married to a very rich man and she cheated on him constantly. She finally actually fell in love with some shlepper and decided it was time to get divorced. Of course she felt so guilty about it all, she settled for very little—and her husband was a multimillionaire. He got married two years later to some gorgeous blonde with big boobs, and he promptly died and left her thirty million. If my friend had hung in there just three more years—which is what you do in the real world—she would've ended up with everything. But no, she had to be Ms. Big Shot, because she had been unfaithful. How many men do you know who would hand over all their money to their wives because they've had a little something on the side?"

Not very many.

Clementine* fell wildly in love with a married man, and he with her—let's call him Winston.* Winston had three children with his wife but was terribly unhappy in the marriage. He left his wife and moved in with Clementine. But very soon, Winston began to feel terribly guilty about leaving his kids. So he left Clementine and went back to his wife. That lasted two years, during which Clementine couldn't bring herself to get interested in anybody else.

Finally, Winston couldn't take it anymore. He left his wife—for good this time—saying that he felt like he was being buried alive. He took with him from the marriage nothing but his toothbrush. He gave his wife everything in the divorce. Winston married Clementine and they started building up again from scratch.

The wife got the money but lost her husband.

Winston got the woman he loved but lost his money.

Clementine got her man but he was penniless.

But truthfully, neither Winston nor Clementine gave a hoot. They were deliriously happy with each other, and felt the money was well spent if it allowed everyone to get on with life. That's what we might call a best possible case, ultracivilized divorce. But they don't all work out that way.

Goodwill is nice, but I wouldn't count on it.

I think we women need a little more protection than that. Of course there are men who are uncommonly decent to their ex-wives, like Winston. The problem is how to distinguish between those who will become rotten during a divorce and those who won't. Don't tell me you "just know" because you don't; you just think you do because you're in love with the man you're about to marry and of course you think the world of him. Just take it from those of us who've been there: The sweetest teddy bear in the world can turn into a monster when it comes time to divvy up the assets.

One in three marriages today ends in divorce. If you plan to travel to a cholera-infested area, you get shots, don't you? Think of a prenuptial as an insurance policy. You hope you never have to use it, but if you do, it's there. You're thrilled you had the foresight to arrange it.

If you're fortunate or careful enough to have one, a prenup saves a lot of wear and tear on everybody. You just do what it says and there's a minimum of fuss. However, if you don't have a prenup, you have to find yourself a good divorce lawyer.

Now, you've probably never hired a divorce lawyer in your life, and you have no idea how to go about finding one. Do you interview them? What do you ask?

Actually, it's very much like choosing a doctor, and you've done that before, so you're not as inexperienced as you think. As with a doctor, you're not really in a position to evaluate the person's qualifications. You don't know the first thing about your surgeon's technique. All you know is whether you feel comfortable with him, whether he has high standing among his peers, and whether he has a good reputation among his patients. In the same way, you don't know what a good affidavit is. You might know that it reads pretty nicely, but does it have all the legal elements necessary to accomplish the purpose in court? It's just like going for a gallbladder operation. Once you're sewed up, if you heal well, you figure the surgeon did a good job, but there's really no way to be absolutely certain.

You can look the lawyer up in the American Academy of Matrimonial Attorneys, but like board certification in medicine, it just means they've passed certain requirements in the field. It doesn't necessarily mean that he or she is the appropriate person for you.

I think you should ask your friends who've been divorced if they were happy with their attorney. Ira Garr disagrees. He says, "A girlfriend might tell you that she did great, she got a four-million-dollar settlement. What she doesn't say and what you don't know is that there was really twenty million dollars there and four million was an inadequate settlement."

But it's a place to start. Get some names and make an

appointment for a consultation. Expect to pay for an hour or two of his/her time.

Come prepared with questions to ask, but also rely on your own reaction when you evaluate the person. This man or woman is going to be important to you. Don't choose somebody whose face you can't abide looking at. Listen to your instincts. If your friend loved so-and-so but his voice raises little prickly hairs on your skin, go elsewhere. If you feel intimidated, or scared, by him or her or if you feel you're not smart enough or are embarrassed because you don't understand legal language, go elsewhere.

There are many competent lawyers around and you have a variety to choose from. Ira Garr compares it to being in a good restaurant: You're in the mood for beef, go with a meat dish. You feel like pasta, have pasta. Whatever you do, you won't go wrong. It's all tasty and well prepared. Unless you live in a very small town, there's more than one lawyer who can do a good job for you. You can simply pick the one you like best from among those you decide are *competent*.

You will want to take notes at that first meeting. If you like, you can even bring along a small tape recorder. That way your hands and your eyes are free to react and respond. You might say something like, "I hope you don't mind if I tape our conversation. I know it's going to be very useful and I'm going to want to refer back to it, and I don't want to get anything wrong."

You'll have your own questions based on the particulars of your case, but here are some questions you should definitely ask the attorney:

• *Who exactly is going to be handling my case? Will I be represented by the firm or an individual?* (Even if you're meeting with the senior partner of the firm, that's no guarantee that he will personally handle your case. As a matter of fact, that meeting may well be the last time you see that senior partner. You may have chosen the firm because of this person's reputation, but the firm may have three hundred lawyers. You don't want to find out that most of your paperwork is being done by somebody one year out of law school. That's not what you've been paying for.)

• *Will you bring in an assistant? If so, what will the assistant do? Are you still going to be in overall control? Will the assistant bill at your rate or his rate? What is his fee per hour?*

• *What's a good time to reach you on the telephone? I understand you're busy and you're in court a lot. Are you reachable at the office between seven and nine in the morning? How about at night?* (You want to know how responsive the attorney will be to you.)

• *Will I get copies of all my papers to the other side?* (Make sure the answer is *yes*. We'll get into the importance of reading everything later.)

• *What is your view on settlement vs. litigation?* (In other words, how much effort will be spent toward exploring a settlement? Of course, no attorney is going to tell you, "I like to litigate and run up big bills" but you can tell if this is one of the attorneys who likes to add fuel to the fire if he seems to be more upset for you than even you are.)

Beware of someone who says things like, "Your husband is the worst piece of garbage I've ever seen. Even *I'm* offended. We're going to make him pay."

What he means is, he's going to make *you* pay.

This "retribution" he's going to exact from your ex-husband is going to be paid for out of the marital estate or, worse, from personal money you might have put aside.

Ira Garr says, "The way I handle it is to say, 'Your husband has done some bad things. I've seen worse. Let's

95

move to the important thing, which is dividing the assets. Or taking care of your children.' I never forget, it's not the husband who's paying, it's the wife, the client. There are lawyers who look for excuses to roll up bigger fees, maybe by bringing out the tank when all that's called for is a peashooter."

• *What are your billing practices?* (Many women feel shy asking about this. Please don't. Not only should you do it, you *must* do it. Otherwise you could wind up in big trouble, not being able to pay for the lawyer in the middle of the action.)

Middle-income couples usually have a joint checking account, but in wealthy circles where there is a substantial amount of money to be managed, the finances are handled by professionals and the woman only has a small checking account, for housekeeping, buying clothes, and so on. The man has the big accounts. He's got access to the real money. He can afford to drag the case on until you just run out of resources, both financially and emotionally.

And all the while he's using *your* money, money that belonged to both of you, money from the matrimonial estate, to pay for *his* lawyers. You might find it hard to get a loan because you don't have a credit rating in your name. You're in a much more difficult position than he is. He knows that and uses it to his advantage.

The lawyer you're consulting will understand this—or should. You might explain that your husband has the assets, but you hope and plan to get your share at the end of the case. Can they make it possible for you to carry on the case until then? Perhaps you can put something down as a retainer, and then make monthly payments. Many lawyers will go along with this since it may be the only way for you to get enough money to pay their fees.

Make sure you get detailed monthly statements, hour by hour. Go over them thoroughly, and if you're not sure what exactly was done on your behalf for all those hours, call and ask. It's only fair. If you don't ask questions you run the risk of being billed over and over again for the same things. If they know you're watching them, they won't dare.

I strongly urge women to try and arrange a flat fee with the lawyer, perhaps by giving him a percentage of the eventual settlement. Otherwise he might try to make things as complicated as possible. There are some lawyers who are always finding "new angles," which translates into another way to increase their hours. But if you decide up front what he will get whether the case takes a month or a year, I guarantee things will go faster. The lawyer has a lot of incentive to finish the case quickly and efficiently. He's more likely to settle since prolonging things won't do him any good. He has no intention of working for the next five years for his money. And he knows that the more he gets you the more he will get. I think that's the most advantageous arrangement for the woman, far better than a "pay by the hour" arrangement.

Legal language is difficult and strange to anyone who's not a lawyer, and legal papers are written in such a way as to make sure there's no chance you could possibly understand them without help.

It's very important that you read all papers that are submitted on your behalf. I don't care if they're boring or difficult or how long it takes. If there's something you don't understand the lawyer is *required* to explain it to you. Take as much time as you need. Don't let anybody rush you or make you feel as if you're bothering them.

Don't let yourself be intimidated.

Ask and ask again about every word, phrase, sentence, or paragraph you don't understand. And if you don't understand the answer, make them explain it again. Go over it until you're sure you understand it. I've gotten myself in lots of trouble because I let things go that I didn't understand. Don't let yourself be intimidated.

Ask, "What does this mean? What does that mean?"

Don't be ashamed or afraid that you are not smart enough. Remember, your lawyer is working for you and taking your money. Let him or her work for it.

You're the one who will be signing your name. If, after all the explanations, you still don't understand the language, make the lawyer change it. Don't ever let anyone intimidate you into signing something you don't understand.

Once lawyers enter the picture, it's no longer just you and your spouse. Each of you has a "handler," a spokesperson, a champion of your cause—and things will never be the same.

By now you can see why I tell divorcing couples that the best advice I can give them is to settle the whole thing between the two of them, if they possibly can. Then all that's necessary is to meet with the lawyers and have them put the agreement into a one-page document, which both parties sign. Do this, and, believe me, you'll be saving a lot of wear and tear on everyone.

May I give you another incentive? Ask yourself whose children you would like to put through school, yours or your lawyer's? Yes, I thought that would get to you.

In order to settle privately, you have to decide what you really want to take with you from this marriage as far as physical possessions go. Please understand that you cannot have it all. This is true whether you have a house in the city and a country house or whether there is only one apartment and it's going to get down to dividing the pots and the TV. You must know what you really want and what you're willing to give up. Would you be happier in the country or do you want to keep the two-bedroom apartment in Manhattan? If you decide to stay in the city, then you'll undoubtedly have to give up the country cottage. If you don't decide what you want you might wind up with the wok when you really wanted the ice bucket.

If you want the TV and the VCR, maybe he takes the stereo. Do be fair.

Please don't fight over every pot and every dish. That gets very painful, not to mention very expensive. "How can that son of a gun take away my lawn mower?" People form passionate attachments to the oddest things, and I guess it only seems odd if it's not your attachment. If you can't work it out yourselves your alternative is to pay huge legal fees to decide who gets the ironing board. Is it worth it?

No, it's not. Give it to him and buy a new one. It'll be much cheaper than paying the lawyers to fight for it.

And when you finally get that settlement, I want you to use it and enjoy it without guilt. We'll talk a little later about how you can learn to manage your money intelligently, but right now I want to make one thing clear: The divorce settlement is not charity. You deserve it. You worked for it, you earned it, and it belongs to you. I think you should have every penny that you're entitled to. And don't let anybody make you feel guilty or money hungry because you're going after it. Where is it written that you have to give up what's fairly yours? As for those people who are criticizing you—how fast would they jump to give up money or property that belongs to them?

Try to get all the money up front, not X amount now and Y at a later date. First of all, it will be easier to close that chapter of your life if you have a lump sum. You can figure out what to do with it, invest it or use it to start a business of your own or whatever.

Secondly, if you have a payment schedule, it keeps you

under his thumb, which is why many men tend to like such an arrangement. This gives a man so many weapons to use: He can stall the payment and make you beg. He can make all kinds of claims to get out of paying. He can force you to go to court to collect, and then pay up at the last second. I had dinner last night with my friend Georgina.* Georgina's been divorced for two years and she didn't get much of a settlement. Instead, they agreed that her husband would be responsible for the maintenance of the household. He would pay for everything she and the children needed.

It sounded all right to her at the time, but, boy, was that a mistake! Only later did she find out that it means every penny she spends has to be okayed by him! And he checks everything! He wants to make sure they're not being spendthrift with "his" money. Furthermore, he thinks everything in the house belongs to him. Georgina told me he wanted some choochoo trains that had been given as gifts to her children. They were antique or something and had some value. But the kids liked them as toys!

I told her to give him the silly trains and tell him to take a long ride. Then he wanted the tools from the garage. This man has three hundred million dollars and he wants those idiotic tools! He can't send his gardener to buy new tools? I told her to throw them out the window and let him pick them up.

Of course, it has nothing to do with the tools themselves. It's a way of keeping control over Georgie. Every time their son wants a pair of Rollerblades, Georgie's ex finds something in the small print to show that Rollerblades weren't included in the agreement. She's got a constant battle on her hands. You can imagine what happens if she wants to take a little ski trip. Oh, no! Too expensive.

She goes through hell.

That's why I'm telling you, honey, get the settlement

and pay for your own ski trip. Otherwise all you have is a lot of aggravation and lawyers who laugh all the way to the bank. Instead of sending your lawyer's kids to private school on what you pay them, buy some certificates of deposit and put the money away for your *own* kids. And if you get the whole settlement at once, you can shake hands and say good-bye nicely; you'll undoubtedly be in touch from time to time to discuss the children. But it's off to your new life!

The larger the marital assets the more complicated the case, of course, and usually it takes a while for the settlement to be worked out and the divorce to be granted. During this period you will be living apart from your husband, but you won't yet be divorced. It's a difficult time, but you'll get through it. The rest of us did, so why shouldn't you?

Chapter 5

Coping Strategies for Your Life Change

*W*hile custody, alimony and child support arrangements, and other legal matters are being worked out, you and your soon-to-be-ex-husband are living apart. The separation period that precedes divorce is a time of confusion and upheaval. Everything is up in the air. You're not really married but you're not divorced. You don't know what to call yourself, you don't know how to introduce yourself. You wear the wedding ring and feel uncomfortable or you *don't* wear the wedding ring and feel uncomfortable.

You're still having trouble getting used to not being part of a couple. You're in limbo socially and romantically. You really can't date anyone, and in any case, you don't feel like dating. This is the period when you're likely to be in your most wounded state, your spirits at their lowest, your heart the most vulnerable.

During this time, you may not even know where you'll be living. Perhaps you'll have to sell the marital home and move somewhere else. But how can you make plans if you don't know how much you can afford? You don't know yet how much money you're going to have. During the separation period, your husband has to give you financial support. Of course, there are always those men who walk out and you never hear from them again, but most do pay up. So there's bread on your table. But we all know that man doesn't live by bread alone, and neither does woman. Here's where you may find your life sadly different from what it was before.

You're cut off from life as you knew it in ways large and small, and often you don't realize it until a door that used to swing open before you on oiled hinges now slams in your face. The country and social clubs in my world can be very snooty and just awful to women who've separated from their husbands. Country club memberships are usually in the man's name; the woman is merely a guest. Suddenly she has nowhere to play golf or tennis or swim or what-have-you. And at this time she needs to exercise and work out more than ever—and probably has an even greater than normal need to get out and see people and have a change of scene.

Social clubs too—like the chic and popular Le Club and Doubles in New York, or Annabel's and Mark's Club in London—may no longer recognize the woman or give her a reservation. She wants to go to lunch with a friend and she finds she can't get into her favorite place. Strange, they loved her there before, when there were two names on her personal checks.

If she tries to join on her own, her ex may very well blackball her. He might plan to bring his dates there and doesn't want to see *her* face across the pool, tennis court, or dining room. Don't expect fairness; the club will side with the member with the most money and power, trust me.

Any change for the worse in your lifestyle is likely to

be magnified at this time because you have very little resilience. Things you might have shrugged off in happier times can loom very large now, since you feel you're about to slide off the end of the earth anyway. These seemingly small things can make life more difficult and uncomfortable than it already is. Your magazine and newspaper subscriptions will run out and it's guaranteed he won't renew them for you. At least you'll have the satisfaction of subscribing in your own name. But you must see to little things like this. You don't want to wind up with nothing to read. You can't allow yourself to sink into lethargy or be any more disconnected from the world than you already are.

I'm perfectly aware that most people can't afford and don't belong to country clubs, but I hear plenty about separated wives being given a hard time, no matter what their financial status. And in cases where there's a considerable marital estate and high-powered lawyers are involved, it becomes hard to concentrate on anything because the lawyers call you a million times a day. As much as you long to get away for a few days, you're afraid to leave town.

You're engaged in a war against someone you loved above all others, with whom you shared everything, up to and possibly including children, and believe me, that takes an emotional toll of its own. Most women are very poorly equipped for this battle. Many of us are just plain frightened of our husbands. This is especially true if he's leaving the marriage for another woman. You worry for the children, you worry for yourself. Your husband was once your most intimate confidant; now he's the adversary. He's unpredictable. He is the enemy. You don't know what he'll do, whom he'll be willing to hurt to get what he wants.

Interestingly, Raoul Felder says that just as women don't seem to have a clear idea of what their husbands do at work, they often have exaggerated ideas of their husband's power. Felder says, "I've seen this time and time again—the least reliable picture of a man comes from his wife. She tells you the husband is this big imposing man, and a schnook walks in. If the husband is a doctor, she thinks he runs the hospital. If he's a bank officer, she thinks he controls the bank. The women perceive the man as large, menacing, and powerful because at home the men push them around."

Raoul, my friend, it's not hard to understand why women see their husbands as powerful, why they build up this image of an all-powerful, invincible foe. It's almost a certainty that of the two partners in the marriage, the husband has nine-tenths of the financial, social, and personal clout.

And when you're going up against him, of course you're afraid. You feel like you've made the worst enemy you'll ever make in your life. And you could be right. Very successful men *are* formidable enemies. They didn't get to be where they are without learning a trick or two. They know who to pay off and how to twist arms and promise favors and generally make things come out the way they want. A wife who has to go up against this kind of man is terribly scared, and she should be! Her fears are perfectly justified.

What can he do to you? I've compiled so many stories from my friends and from letters women wrote me.

He can destroy your day with just one phone call. He knows just which buttons to push to make you miserable. After all, you were together for years. He knows what upsets you, where your sensitive spots are, what will get your back up. (You probably can do the same to him. You just can't seem to hold a conversation without hurting each other.) Many lawyers forbid you to talk to the man for strategy reasons, but some don't. They advise against it, but they leave it up to you. "Why speak to this man," they say, "if every time you do you get hysterical?" Of course, this good advice makes the lawyers a lot of money because now you and your husband have to communicate via legal letters instead.

Fortunately, there are things you can do. You can simply not pick up the phone if you know he's in a filthy mood. Let the phone ring—or let him rant and rave to the answering machine. Or it might help to put your mother or sister or a close friend on the line. A third party often makes people control themselves. They don't want to be seen as a flaming idiot by someone else.

Another "technique" women are familiar with is having the man "somehow" manage to have papers served on you just before a holiday. Nothing spoils the fun of a holiday faster than finding out there's some new legal action against you. Maybe the kids mentioned a weekend getaway, so their father knows you're looking forward to a little break, a little rest and recuperation, and bingo, you get served with papers. Your blood instantaneously starts to boil, your pressure goes up . . . and your vacation fizzles out.

One man I know called his wife at about 4:45 in the afternoon on April 15 to advise her that he wasn't filing jointly with her this year, she was on her own. He really had her going—she was terribly upset. Since she'd never dealt with tax returns before, she never dreamed that all she had to do was file for an extension. That's one of the reasons I want to see you well set up in the technical areas of accounting and financial advice.

How will men hurt you? Let me count the ways.

If he finds out you have a boyfriend, he might try to say that you are an unfit mother. He might even say that the child was looking on while you had sex. Nothing is too dreadful for a man to throw at you, I'm sorry to say. He might be especially prone to using this as a weapon if he knows how much you adore your kids. While I've known fathers who were nuts about their kids, in my experience it's the woman who really wants custody and the man who threatens to take it from her. Most of the time they don't even want the children. God forbid you should give them to him! It's far too much hassle for men. Even if they're going to leave the children to housekeepers and nannies, they still have to deal with hiring them, and that's not easy. All they really want is to upset the ex-wife. And usually a threat to take the kids away is more than enough to drive any woman out of her mind.

A friend of mine was spotted leaving her house with a suitcase. Well, clearly she was having an affair —isn't that obvious to you? In actuality, it was a business trip, and she did not leave the children unsupervised. But that's the kind of unfair accusation you may have to contend with. And if he doesn't think of it, his lawyer might help him to "see" it.

Or, he might do something to scuttle your business deals or otherwise try to mess up something you're about to achieve. Very often this kind of tactic will succeed because the world is so competitive and many situations are delicate to begin with. Business deals are so fragile, the merest whisper of trouble is enough to destroy them. The facts hardly matter, it's enough that there's someone around wishing you ill. The last thing anyone needs is to "get in bed," as the Wall Street types put it, with someone who's got an unhappy ex lurking in the background.

Very often the man is extremely unreasonable and may not consciously know the reason why: He can't stand the idea that you're going to walk away from this in one piece. He may be very threatened by the fact that you're a survivor.

Be doubly and triply discreet and look at every move you make with an eye to how it might be used against you. If he has means and enough curiosity or ill will, your husband may have people in his employ watching you. Suspect your staff unless you can be absolutely sure of them. If your maid worked for your mother, your sister, and your cousin, she's probably okay. But who has that kind of staff these days?

If you have a once-a-week housekeeper or cleaning woman, I wouldn't be surprised if your ex asks her to come do his apartment. After all, she's probably the only one he knows. I'm not saying you have to be suspicious of everybody—but be alert, be careful. Don't let her see or hear anything you wouldn't like passed on to him. If she's honorable and doesn't report to him, you haven't lost anything. But these women don't make a lot and don't have a lot and if he's waved a few extra dollars in her face, she might just be tempted. Better safe than sorry.

You may get the feeling that every time you're about to work out your life your ex finds a way to prevent you or something nasty happens between you. If so, see if you can find a pattern. Then you'll be able to take steps to avoid it. A woman wrote that her husband would always do something terrible to her just before her period. He knew her menstrual cycle, he knew when she would be edgy, hyper, and likely to overreact, and that's when he would serve legal papers or haul her into court.

Simple but clever.

When she caught on, the woman went to her doctor and asked how to change her cycle. He gave her pills that she had to take for a certain number of days, and they brought on her period, which put her on a totally different cycle. This woman's menstrual period changed from mid-month to the beginning of the month or whatever, and when her husband hauled her into court, she was full of spunk and energy and ready to go after him like a tiger. Don't you love that?

By the way, men also have a blind spot regarding their wives, only with them it involves virtue, not finances. My research showed that one difference between the sexes is that while women think their husbands are *all-powerful*, men think their wives are completely *faithful*. Raoul Felder told me a great story:

"We represented one fellow in my office whom we called 'My wife, never.' You see, he had fallen in love with another woman and his wife wouldn't give him a divorce. We suggested he have her followed. 'My wife? Never.' He said it so many times, we began to call him that. When we talked about him in the office, we didn't use his name, we'd say, 'My wife? Never,' as in 'Get My Wife Never on the phone for me, please.'

"He was going out of town on a business trip. We convinced him to put detectives on his wife. Just for fun, we said. We know she'd *never* do anything wrong.

"Well, we didn't have to wait long. The very first night he was away, the wife exited the home wearing a hot-to-trot miniskirt topped off by a rhinestone-studded cowboy hat. For seven nights the detectives followed her on dates with five different men. One of them was the pediatrician who lived next door."

Doesn't it seem that men often think it natural to run around as much as they want, but if their wives have an affair, they go nuts? And they don't see anything illogical or unfair about it. I've mentioned this to several lawyers and they all said the same thought had crossed their minds.

Women tell me how ashamed and embarrassed they felt when they were first separated from their husbands. They couldn't even face their mother, let alone the church and the community. What is everyone going to think? To them I say: Don't worry about what your neighbor thinks. It doesn't matter. You have to face the reality that the man is gone. You have to think of what you're going to do, plan ahead, pull yourself together, pull the kids together. Don't worry about the neighbors (or in my case, the newspapers) because there is nothing in the world you can do about it.

Of course it hurts. It hurts like hell. It was during this separation period that I remembered hearing something about an ex-wife being the most pathetic creature on earth, somebody fit just to slink off into the shadows.

That's not for me. I wasn't put on this earth to be invisible. I had no intention of becoming a nonperson, thank you very much.

But what to do? I started to think. I started to plan. I said, All right, I can't work at the Plaza much longer. It's best for all concerned if I don't work for my ex-husband. But I stayed on for several months, using that time to answer letters, firm up contacts, etc. Using your old job to get your new one is a classic technique.

I knew that with my experience managing the hotels and casinos in Atlantic City and the Plaza Hotel in New York, I could probably get a job in hotel management at a very handsome salary with no problem. But I didn't want to work in the same field that I had while I was married. I didn't want anyone to be able to claim credit for my success, to be able to say, "I taught her all she knows." I had to branch out into new fields.

Do you know the old saying, "When God closes a door He opens a window"? It was just at this time that the proposal was put before me that I should write a novel. I'd never done it before, but I thought: How about that. Maybe I should.

And approaches were made to me about the Ivana signature line of clothing, jewelry, and cosmetics that I'm now selling on the Home Shopping Network. And I had started to spend considerable time traveling around the country on speaking engagements.

Now's a good time to introduce you to Ivana's Important Rule Number 1: Never look back. Only forward.

There's absolutely nothing you can do about the past and so much you can do about the future.

Stop worrying about what he wants and get what you need for yourself and your children. You've done what he wants for fifteen years, or whatever. (It only *seems* like a hundred.) Let his new woman worry about his needs. This is a time for you to be a little bit selfish.

It was difficult trying to plan a future while the lawyers were fighting back and forth, and that took up a lot of time and energy. That's one of the reasons that I say the divorce finally comes as a relief. I think you have to find a way to take all this anger, pain, and frustration and use that energy in a positive way, by working on yourself and your future. We all know of cases where the wife uses the children against her ex-husband. She takes legal action to prevent the father from seeing his children, or moves away to another state. She gets her revenge on him, but who really gets hurt? The kids do. They lose their father. The children haven't done any of those terrible things to you. So be very careful not to put them in the middle of your fight with him.

It may be hard to restrain yourself, given some of the things your ex might do to harass you, but my feeling is you simply have to get a grip on yourself and not sink to his level.

Right here, where I'm saying so many awful things about men, I want to make it very clear that I am not someone who doesn't like men. I adore men! They're the champagne on the wine list of life. I'm always happier when I have a man in my life and a little forlorn without one. After all, that's the way we are made, isn't it? But the fact that I appreciate men and need to love them doesn't mean I ignore some of the perfectly dreadful things some men do to women, especially in the course of a divorce.

I must say, things do seem to improve. I think we learn

to make better choices. The man I'm with now is perfectly delicious, aside from being very supportive and unthreatened by my work and fame. On the contrary, he gets a kick out of what I do and cheers me on. Honestly, it's a whole new world, and one that I enjoy very much.

And it would never have happened if I hadn't gotten a divorce. Just think, I wouldn't have met Riccardo, wouldn't have written my books or done all the different things I'm doing. If I were still married to my ex-husband, I promise you I wouldn't have my contract with the Home Shopping Network to sell my Ivana line of clothing, jewelry, and cosmetics.

In a way, my father's death precipitated my divorce.

I had had the divorce papers prepared about a week after the incident in Aspen, but they hadn't been filed. The lawyers advised me to get a settlement first, then I'd be in a better position to get the divorce, and I said, maybe so, but have the papers ready.

My father, Miloš Zelníček, had been in exceptional health all his life when he died suddenly of a heart attack at sixty-four. I can't help but feel it was brought on by stress, specifically the stress of my divorce. He had never been ill in his life. He was a champion skier and swimmer, he exercised every day. My dad was full of life. He would dance till four in the morning.

As soon as we got the news, my children and I flew to Czechoslovakia, where he had been at the time of his death. His loss was terribly hard for all of us to bear—myself, my mother, the children. My kids were especially close to him—he was a wonderful grandfather—and I felt it was somehow unfair since they had been through so much that year.

All the while we were making the arrangements and all through the funeral, I kept thinking what a miserable, horrible year it had been. I wanted to put it behind me as fast as I could.

At the graveside, while we were burying my father, I saw there were photographers from all over the world. They watched every step my family and I made at this most private and personal of moments. To this day I don't know how they found out when and where the funeral was, in this teeny little town in Czechoslovakia.

It was then that I made the decision to file the divorce papers. I didn't care anymore what was strategically clever or wise. Even though I wasn't yet divorced legally, I was divorced emotionally. I had been going my own way, and in the meantime, things were starting to drag with lawsuits, appeals. Who knew if the financial settlement would take five years? I wanted to start to see other people but I didn't want to date while I was married. I didn't want to give my ex any ammunition, nor did I want anybody to be able to say that I had fooled around during my marriage.

And there was another reason I wanted to be divorced. I'm a religious woman. I go to church. I couldn't see being married to one man and dating others; separated or no, I was still a married woman. For me, morally, it made a difference.

It had been the worst year of my life. My father's funeral seemed a good time to say, let's scratch this year— put it away, don't think about it. Start all over again.

There was a new year coming and I wanted to start with a clean slate.

Within fourteen days, I had my divorce.

Chapter 6

Helping Your Children Adjust

*O*ne of the worst things about the breakup of a marriage is what it does to children: It robs them of their rightful childish innocence. They gave their father complete and unquestioning trust and he betrayed them. At least, that's the way they see it in most instances—and in a case like Ashley's, below, they're right. How else can they see it?

I have been reading a lot about you and Mr. Trump lately. I'm eleven years old and in the sixth grade. About one year ago my Mom went by a local restaurant at 6 P.M. [and] in the parking lot was my father's van. She and her friend went inside the restaurant and what should they find but my father with another woman. She confronted them and my father just didn't say anything, but his girlfriend did. She said, I'm sorry (in a very cold voice) but he doesn't love you anymore. He loves me. My Mom burst out in tears. She walked out of the restaurant sobbing. I would also like to add that my father never took us out to eat. He said it was too expensive. But he and her were eating appetizers! A couple of months later on Valentine's Day we wanted to know where he was living, so we went by his girlfriend's house and he was there [with] all his clothes lined out neatly and they were getting ready to go out to eat! They go out every night! Well my Mom and him had it out and then he told her he hated her. We left and I didn't go to school the next day. This year my parents got divorced on Valentine's Day. But nobody told me until three days later. My Mom found out that my Dad got married to his mistress the day after he and my mother had gotten divorced. He also took her on a week's honeymoon! He never took my Mom anywhere! This made me very mad because he didn't even tell me he was getting married. I had to find out for myself. I haven't seen him for a year now! And I don't believe he loves or cares about me anymore or if he ever did. My father now has two stepchildren whom he buys whatever they want! He doesn't even pay child support! So it is a constant struggle for money. I am a very good student who makes excellent grades and I have blond hair and blue-green eyes. I'm not fat or ugly. So I don't understand why my father doesn't love me. I have lots of friends and hang out with the popular crowd.

My Mom now has a boyfriend who lives with us and has been more of a father to me than my real father ever was. My whole family and I all think that you are much more beautiful than Mr. Trump's girlfriend. She takes dorky pictures. A woman of your great beauty will be sure to find a man who hopefully will treat you better. I hope I have made you feel better now that you know that you're not alone. Don't worry, it gets better.

Ashley

Oh, my goodness, that letter leaves me not knowing if I want to laugh or cry; this eleven-year-old darling trying to reassure me and make me feel better? I feel so much for her.

Did you notice how she searches body and soul for a defect with which to explain her father's abandonment? Children can be so wise and yet so naive at the same time. The father's secret affair, found out by accident; the confrontation with the mistress; the cold statement "He doesn't love you anymore; he loves me." Notice how much better the father treats his mistress than his wife: They go out to dinner every night. Could he spare something for his children? Not according to this letter.

What children need most is someone they can trust, someone they can rely on, and unfortunately, that person is you. I say "unfortunately" because you're not exactly feeling like the Rock of Gibraltar yourself these days. But you are all they have. I know you feel like falling apart yourself, but you've got to think of your kids first just now; you must find it in yourself to be strong for them. Amid your own turmoil, you must find strength for them.

They know something's wrong. They can't help but sense the tension. The child rattles the silverware at dinner, and you blow up. You're under stress, your nerves are stretched taut. Little things set you off.

How will you find the strength? I'm not sure, but I believe you will. It helps to keep in mind that if you feel hopeless and despairing, the children will know it and if you panic, so will they. It will lead to all kinds of unfortunate circumstances; it can affect their schoolwork, their friendships, everything.

> Jeremy who was never afraid of anything is afraid of the dark since his parents broke up.
>
> Gail

Somehow, you have to avoid showing your children that you're scared. You have to dig deep and find the courage to protect them. I know there are times when you're going to fall apart, but try to do it when they're at school or out of the house. Think about how terrifying it must be to have your father betray you and your mother go to pieces at the same time.

They must be bewildered enough as it is, with all the changes going on that probably nobody has explained to them. The first thing you must do is tell them the truth. I don't mean sharing every gory detail of every sexual exploit with them. No! But you have to tell them that their father will no longer be living with them. He has fallen in love with somebody else (or whatever will fit your personal scenario) and he will go to live with her (or by himself). But please stress as forcefully as you can: "He will always be your father. *We* are divorcing, not you."

It's best, of course, if you and your spouse can sit down and tell the kids together. That's the most reassuring for them and they will have reason to believe you when you tell them that their lives will stay pretty much the same and their relationships with each of you won't change. But this isn't always possible. You can't control what their father will or won't say, but you can make yourself an "honest broker" for them. They will learn in time that from you they get the truth (even if it's a little shaded for their benefit) and they will know whom they can trust.

No matter how the marriage breaks up, children almost invariably feel that they can make you get back together if they can only figure out how. This is their fondest wish—unless their father has abused them, in which case they may feel mostly relief to know that they won't live with him anymore and are safe from him.

You have to make them understand that they have no choice in the matter, and no voice in the decision. Nothing they say or do can change it. They didn't bring it about and they can't stop it from happening.

Don't tell the children *anything* until your decision is

firm and irreversible: What a shame to put them through it only to have you reconcile, or back out, or simply change your mind twenty-four hours later.

If it isn't a sudden break, and you have the time, you can prepare them slowly. The children will know you're unhappy. They hear you crying. They know you haven't slept—they're aware of you walking around the house in the middle of the night. They may have heard you and your husband fighting. Don't think they don't notice or that it goes over their heads. It doesn't, believe me. Children are very sensitive where their parents are concerned. You'll be much closer to the truth if you *over*estimate rather than underestimate how much they know.

A good time to have this talk is when they've already alluded to it. If you can, pick a time when they've either said something or done something relating to your marital troubles. My children were often especially affectionate to me during this time, which is typical.

If your children do something unusually caring, or come for an unexpected snuggle in your lap, they might be trying to let you know that they're aware and they care. This would be a good time to bring the subject up. You might say something like, "I guess you know that Daddy and I aren't getting along very well right now."

Kids learn about divorce in nursery school these days and they will probably ask you if you're going to get a divorce. Tell them that you haven't decided anything yet (if that's the case) but you won't do anything without letting them know.

If you feel you can patch your marriage up, you might emphasize how hard you and Daddy are going to work to stay together. But make it very clear to them that they *will be told* if and when it happens. That way they don't have to waste any energy wondering.

Try to get across to them that they have no input, no responsibility, and can have no effect on what happens.

It's not easy: Children almost always seem to think the opposite, but you have to try to convince them otherwise.

Encourage your children to come to you and tell you if their playmates speak of the divorce. When they do—or even if they don't—ask them what the other children say. Then you can help your children prepare answers. I find that "rehearsing" a child helps a lot. Play-act the situation with them. Pretend you're on the playground or whatever and you take the part of another child. Say something like, "Is it true your daddy isn't your daddy anymore?" If your child has told you of some specific remarks, then use those.

Then help your child frame a reply: "My parents are getting a divorce. They didn't want to be a family with each other anymore because they couldn't get along. So they're not going to live in the same house. But my daddy is still my daddy. Nothing will change that."

Of course you tailor the "rehearsal" to your child's age and the specific circumstances of your separation.

> My boyfriend is a wealthy man with small children. One day when they were with us for their weekend visitation, I walked into Susie's room and she was crying. I asked her what was wrong and she told me, "Mommy hates half of me and Daddy hates the other half."
>
> Angie

Somehow children always blame themselves for the divorce: "If I were a better boy or girl, Daddy would still love us and live with us." Remember how bewildered Ashley was that her dad left *even though* she was pretty and got good grades? It doesn't seem to cross her mind that the fault might lie with her mother *or* her father. No. It was clear to her that *she* had caused this, and she could make her daddy come back and everything would be the way it was . . . if only she could figure out how.

You have to work hard to disabuse your children of this idea. You bring it up, even if they don't, because if they haven't followed this line of thinking, I'll be surprised.

You might say something like, "Many children think that their parents got divorced because of something they did, they were naughty or something. Do you ever think that?"

Even if the child says no, I'd go on: "Divorce is something that happens to grownups. Grownups get divorces, not children. It has nothing to do with children. They don't make it happen and they can't stop it from happening."

You might use simple examples: "Can you drive a car? No. You're just simply too young. Remember when we went to the amusement park and there were rides you couldn't go on because you weren't tall enough? Divorce is like that. It's not for children your age to worry about or have anything to do with."

I have to tell you that no matter how many times you say this, it still may not sink in. Someone told me about a little girl whose parents have been divorced since she was two and she's now almost seven. Her mother is a teacher and has repeated this conversation over and over again with the daughter.

And guess what the child tells her friends? "My daddy and mommy broke up because I was bad and they got mad at me."

Aside from the sadness she feels for her daughter, this woman is ready to climb the walls! How many times in how many ways can she tell this girl that it is *not her fault?!*

Which just goes to show you how powerful that idea is. Children hear what they hear. So you have to keep trying.

You can expect your children to feel very angry, very frightened, and, in general, as if their world were crumbling about them.

Sound familiar? Yes . . . they feel everything you feel. But they're not verbal enough to express their feelings in words, so they act out their emotions in various ways. Unusual fears are very common: A child suddenly won't get on the bus or sleep through the night or whatever. You may find that children's grades drop or they become aggressive and get into fights. Or they go the other way and become closed off and withdrawn.

That's one reason why you have to pull yourself together. If you're in bad shape, coming apart at the seams, you won't be able to give them much help or direction, will you?

My children were with me when that incident happened in Aspen, so to some extent they were in on it from the beginning. Upset as I was, I didn't want to panic them, so I told them I felt sure there was some misunderstanding and I would work it out with their father.

Before I sat them down for a talk, I had to try and put things into perspective for myself. I couldn't have any kind of serious conversation with them until I had a chance to sort out my own feelings.

Of course I was very upset, and the kids knew it. But I couldn't be reassuring to them because I was in a state of panic myself. My children knew that something terrible was happening, but they didn't ask about it directly. This is not unusual. Children are often too scared to bring it up themselves. But I could see that they knew in the way they behaved toward me: so tender and caring—especially my eldest son, Donny. He stayed at my side the whole time. He even sat up all night with me one night when I was too upset to sleep.

After a while, it became clear that my marriage was over. I waited until we had actually separated before I sat the kids down for a talk. By then, my main emotion was relief, if the truth be known. To me nothing is worse than a state of chaos and upheaval. I'd much rather know what I have to deal with; then I can get on and deal with it.

I remember being very calm when I had this conversation, and I'm sure it was better that I waited until I felt I could manage it without breaking down. However, you can't wait *too* long because the children will surely hear it from somewhere else. How awful it would be if they were to find out from a classmate who heard it from his parents who heard it from . . . ? You know how it goes.

I explained to my kids that their father had met somebody else and we were separating. I told them that it was better for us to live apart rather than to be unhappy.

But I made sure to tell them that "even though your father has left, nothing else will change in your life. You will go see him someplace else, but you will go on living in the same house, the same bedroom. You will have the same toys, the same schools, we will take the same vacations. Your grandparents will love you just as they did before, and you will be with them just as much.

"Your father and I will be getting a divorce but *you're* not getting a divorce from him. Your father will still be your father. You can see him anytime you want, for as long as you want. We will go on living in this apartment, we will drive the same car, you will have all your toys and clothes and computers and whatever."

(Those little details mean so much to children. It's the structure of their lives.)

I don't think you can stress too much, as I did over and over: "The divorce is between me and your father, not either one of us and you. You still have the same parents and the same grandparents. You don't have to take sides—I don't *want* you to take sides."

During this rather difficult time, I tried to keep everything as normal as possible around them, but of course it was hard to do since the children couldn't help seeing the whole story on every newsstand they passed and on every nightly news show. I instructed the nanny not to put the television on. Our house rule is not to watch television during the week anyway, so they didn't find it unusual.

Over and over I told them none of this was their fault.

Of course their teachers and friends were reading the newspapers and watching television too. I spoke to each of the children's teachers and headmasters when my marriage broke up, and after that I made it a point to stay in touch with them. I'd give them a call every now and then to see how my children were handling the situation. I think you should do the same. Don't feel you're bothering the teacher or the principal. That's their job.

Unfortunately, all the care and intelligence in the world won't stop children from reacting to your divorce. And if you think about it, why shouldn't they react to what's happened?

Your goal is to get them through it with the least amount of trauma. But I don't think it's possible to stop them entirely from feeling the pain and heartbreak, no matter how much you wish you could.

And we all know that children can be very cruel to each other. The headmaster of Donny's school called me and said we had a problem at school: Donny had gotten into a fight with two students in a higher grade and apparently he'd beaten the daylights out of them—both of them.

I said, "That's not like Donny. He's a real gentleman. What did the two boys do to him or say to him, because I feel sure they must have done something to provoke him."

I was right. Apparently the kids had made some remark about me and my marital situation. I don't know exactly what, because Donny wouldn't repeat it to me, but heaven knows they had *a lot* of inspiration from the newspapers. So Donny beat the you-know-what out of them.

I told the headmaster, "I'm going to speak with Donny

because I don't approve of violence and I don't want him beating up half the school. But if somebody said that to me, I'd beat them up too and I'm proud of him for standing up for me and for his family."

I told Donny the same thing when I spoke to him, that I understood why he did it and that I was proud of him. However, I also told him that this is not the way, that he had to learn to ignore this kind of thing. I said: "I know it's hard and those boys were mean and nasty. Don't show that you're upset. Don't give them the satisfaction of knowing they got to you."

That was the end of it. It never happened again.

But that didn't mean Donny wasn't affected by our divorce. That was the time when we were looking for a boarding school for him. We visited several and he had found one he liked. I encouraged him to enroll for the following year. If he wanted to go, it was perfectly okay with me. He thought about it for about a week and finally said, "Mom, I don't think I'll go to boarding school this coming year."

"Why not? You were dying to go."

"I think you need me around right now."

Well—I cried. He was already trying to "replace" the man in my life, protecting me and caring for me. I told him, "Donny, I do need you. But I can manage without you for a little while." I told him over and over he could go, but he wound up staying home one more year and enrolled the year after that. Can you see why I adore him? And why I feel so blessed when I think of any of my children?

Ivanka was very brave during our family crisis—she was so dignified! The teacher told me it was incredible how she handled herself. Not only didn't her marks slide, she worked even harder and got even better grades.

However, I know she didn't escape without problems. Kids can be very cruel, and probably they were jealous of her to some extent all along and it came out now. She didn't say much. All she would tell me was that so-and-so was mean. But I could fill in the rest for myself. I must say I'm very proud of her. She kept her head high and went about her business.

Eric had some difficulties. There was so much on his mind that it interfered with his concentration. I knew he was worried about me. I spoke to his teacher, and we tried to think of strategies to release some of his tension. His eyes would be out the window, he'd lose the thread of a conversation, and his teacher would say, "Eric!"— and he would come back. That would happen three or four times a day.

I didn't blame him for being distracted. He was living in a nightmare that went on twenty-four hours a day, without letup. He is the youngest and didn't understand fully what was going on. I realized that I simply had to get the children away, and that's when I took them to Mar-a-Lago in Florida. It was only a couple of weeks till spring break anyway and at least there I could be sure they weren't reading newspapers. In New York, even if I kept the papers out of the house, they would see them somehow. Mar-a-Lago is a large property and the children were totally insulated there from the hysteria surrounding their father and me.

The kids were out of school for about two months altogether, but I had a tutor for them. I spoke to each of their teachers before we left, and they were more than understanding. They faxed me the children's homework every day.

Usually, I have a houseful of kids when I'm down in Palm Beach. But this time, I didn't let my children bring anybody along, not even a best friend. I didn't want anybody going home and talking about us. I was even cautious about the staff. I didn't want them telling the tabloids what went on in the house, even something as simple and innocuous as "Ivana had friends in for dinner." Nobody except my maid was allowed to come into my room. I didn't want anybody overhearing my conversations on the telephone. We had very few guests that month, and those few were people I could trust not to ask questions or bring up certain subjects.

But the most important thing was that the children were with family, including my parents. My father was still alive then and both he and my mother adored the kids, and the feeling was mutual. And of course, Mar-a-Lago is heaven. The children couldn't help but have a great time. They went swimming and played tennis every day; they went to the beach, they went fishing. They didn't miss their friends at all. They had each other.

What counted most of all, they knew I was taking care of them. The children understood exactly why we were there, and why we didn't have friends with us. You have to walk a fine line. With friends you have to be careful what you say, but you can't be so suspicious that you lose them. You have to trust . . . but not too much. But with family you don't have to be guarded. You can tell them anything. They are there for you, they're on your side. They want to help you. My parents helped me and my children enormously. My kids adore them both, and they still miss my father, who died the following October, very much.

You have to be very careful when you speak to children of their father. It's very important that you not give children the idea that their father is "bad" or that you hate him. He is their father—the only one they will ever have. And your children are half their father and half you. If he is worthless, then so are they.

But you have to tell them *something* if he's not acting right toward them. What if he's really being miserable? What can you say that won't hurt the children?

The best you can do is tell them that people sometimes behave in ways that are not good. Sometimes they do wrong things that might hurt others. This is a fact of life.

You can acknowledge the wrongs their father has done, but be careful not to say nasty things about *him* no matter how angry you are or how tempted you might be or what cause he gives you. Bite your lips. Clench your fists. Leave the room if you must. But never forget that he's their father. Not to mention they'll likely tell him what you said and he'll try twice as hard to get back at you.

This next point is a little more subtle and a little more difficult: Try to make sure that your children never catch you speaking badly of their father when you're talking to someone else—on the phone, let's say. I find children frequently listen to the conversation that's on their end, even if only half-consciously. The temptation to unload on a friend or a sister or your mother might be very great, and you forget to guard your tongue because you're not talking to the child. But the child is listening nonetheless.

Your kids know their daddy has hurt you. Sometimes they feel guilty about spending time with him, or even wanting to spend time with him. I didn't tell my children whether or not to spend time with their father. I said, "If you want to go anytime, all you have to do is say the word. It's your decision. If you don't want to go, that's okay too. All this will straighten out eventually."

And it did. Everyone calmed down. The children began to see that their mother was going on with her life. She wasn't panicking; their lives hadn't changed drastically. They stopped being so nervous.

In general, except to your closest relatives and friends, I think it's best not to say anything bad about your husband at any time. He's your children's father, and any mud you fling at him will cling a little to them.

However, if your husband is behaving in a *very* neglectful and hurtful way to the children, I don't feel that you should try to convince them that he still loves them. They can see it's not true. Even a small child knows that if you love someone you don't abandon them and otherwise treat them badly. This is a tricky situation, I admit, and I'm not sure anything you do will be one hundred percent correct. It's plain tough to explain some of the things men have been known to do. Try to walk a fine line between the harsh truth on the one hand and being negative about their father on the other hand.

If he still sees them, let *him* try to explain his behavior. If he can.

However, it's more likely the father will *not* abandon his children completely in favor of his stepchildren, or for any other reason. He most likely will continue a relationship with them in one form or another. Usually, the way it works out is that he has visitation rights, which means that he takes them for certain weekends, some holidays, and perhaps a longer block of time during the year, during summer vacation or Christmas break.

Today coparenting or joint custody is becoming more and more popular. The child spends some time with each parent. He or she has a room, toys, clothes, etc., in each place. That can work out well, but the parents have to live very close to each other and the child's school and friends so that the child is equally "at home" in both places. I don't think it would work well if the child had to make a separate group of "at home" friends for three or four days a week and on alternate weekends. However, if the child has the same play dates and after-school activities it can work—with a lot of goodwill on both sides, needless to say. But then again, goodwill is invaluable in all divorces, and that goes double when there are children involved.

School reports are usually sent to both of you separately, at your respective addresses. Both parents are invited to attend parent-teacher conferences. You can mutually agree to arrive separately and speak to the teacher separately if you don't feel you can handle it together.

Recitals and plays and such can be difficult. You're both in the same place at the same time and if your divorce has caused any kind of public interest, this is everyone's chance to stare.

Here's what I do—and I'll bet you can make this trick work for you, too. Since our nanny wants to see the children performing or reciting too, she always comes with us to events like these. I have her get there early to hold seats for us in the first row. I come in exactly on time and take my seat. There's no rule that I have to turn around to see people who are behind me. I don't have to look anywhere but the stage. You can do the same thing. Have someone save your seat—your sister, a friend, whoever. If you do have to pass him, just say hi, and go on your way.

Please resist the temptation to take this chance to give him a piece of your mind. Don't give everyone the satisfaction of seeing you quarrel in public. You want to stay on a certain level in your dealings with him and with everyone else. In any case, this is your child's day and you want to make it as easy and pleasant as possible for him or her.

If you really can't abide seeing your husband—and many people feel that way at least for half a year or so—then you have to stay away. Make an appointment to go to the classroom another time, to see the artwork or whatever, and to speak to the teacher. You're trying to let the child know that you care, even if you won't be at the class picnic or sporting event.

Last year we had to go to some kind of picnic at Eric's school. It was between five and seven in the evening. My secretary called my ex-husband's secretary and told her that I would go from five to six. Therefore he knew that a good time for him to go was between six and seven.

I'm not saying your ex will always respect this, but it's good to try. If he does come while you're there, you should be cordial and polite. He can probably guess what you're really thinking, but the rest of the world doesn't have to know.

I believe in keeping your dignity—for your children's sake and for your own. If you run him down you run yourself and your children down. You married him. You had children with him. If he's the worst human being that ever lived, what does that make you? And your children, the product of this marriage?

If you have a son, you hope he'll learn positive ways of treating women even if he's angry with them. And if you have daughters, you want them to comport themselves with dignity no matter how hurt they are. So you have to be their role model.

It's very easy to make the children into spear carriers in your war with your husband: "Tell that so-and-so . . ." But your children are not messengers and won't be any happier for delivering the unpleasant words you've sent via them. You have a lawyer. His job is to be the bearer of evil tidings. Don't lay this on your kids.

So many of my friends told me they had used the children as go-betweens: Tell Mommy this, tell Daddy that. I think if you do that, you're putting your children in an awful situation.

What if your ex does that? You might do as I did, and prepare the children with a stock answer to give in that situation. I told my children that if their father asked them anything about me, they should simply say, Dad, please don't get us involved. If you want to know something about Mommy, why don't you ask her? I love you and I love Mommy and I'm not going to get in the middle of it.

And by the way, assume that when they're with him, they talk about you and your doings. It's only natural and it would be foolish of you to expect otherwise. After all, you don't want them to have to guard their tongues at all times. Are you raising children or secret agents? What they know will probably come out, so don't let them know what you don't want them to speak of.

Visitation rights are agreed to between you and your ex-spouse and they set up an automatic schedule which you are both supposed to follow, but I think you have to be a little flexible. Don't make a fuss about trivial things. You won't impress him with how powerful you are and you'll just upset the kids. I really don't care if the children are a half hour late coming back from their weekend with my ex-husband. It's not worth getting excited over. I'd much rather greet them with a kiss than with a fight.

What really messes you up is if he doesn't tell you until the last minute that he *doesn't* plan to take them on his weekend. You were going to go away, and suddenly all your plans are ruined. Even though I have a nanny living with us, and my mother lives with us eight months out of the year so that there is always someone in the house, I can't very well go to Paris when I know the children are home without plans. I'd feel too guilty, and you would too.

Look, this man probably wasn't the most considerate person in the world before your divorce and I doubt you're going to teach him new tricks now. I sometimes wonder how men can casually say, "I'm not going to take the kids this weekend" and not feel guilty. It's the woman who either drops everything and changes her plans or makes sure to have alternate arrangements. At my house, we plan that the children will go to our country place in Greenwich each weekend and if we don't hear from their father by late afternoon on Friday, they're in the car and on their way, no pressure, nobody's angry at anybody. If he calls and takes them, wonderful. If not, they're not crushed, because their weekend wasn't disrupted.

Don't be surprised if your ex doesn't want to be married to you but still wants to control you. And the easiest way for him to do that is through the children. This is so typical it should almost be expected.

Here are some common ways the control freak operates:

• He wants the kids to visit *his* mother on Mother's Day. The kids naturally *want* to be with you and you want them. You're their mother; he has his.

• He wants to take them out on school nights. He always picks someplace that the kids are dying to go, but naturally, they don't get home till after eleven. He doesn't have to get them up for school the next morning. He doesn't have to deal with tantrums and tears from lack of sleep, or missed school buses, forgotten lunches, and undone homework. This is called making a mess and letting someone else clean it up.

• The kids mention that nice man who spent the afternoon with all of you in the park. Your ex hauls you into court to explain your "cohabitation" and makes you fight for your alimony all over again. (If your friend spends time doing that invaluable male-bonding stuff with your sons, that will probably infuriate your ex even more. *He* hasn't found the time to take the kids to the park but he certainly doesn't want someone else doing what *he* should be doing.)

The "control freak" can make you want to scream. One of my girlfriends had a big blowup with her ex over a lousy baseball bat. The husband wanted to know why the kid needed a new one. Because he did, that's why! He'd grown since he got the last one and it was too small. The husband gave her so much grief over that lousy bat she nearly exploded. Her husband could buy the whole *stadium* if he felt like it. This isn't about money. It's about control: "He'll get a new bat when I say he needs one, not when you do."

None of this is spoken, but it's there under the surface nevertheless. There's no great way to deal with this except to interact with the control freak as little as possible. You're not going to change him. You couldn't while you were married, so you sure can't now.

No matter what kind of strain there is between you, I think that when your husband has the kids you have to be a good soul and keep him from falling flat on his face. Men usually know very little about the daily routine the children follow. They know the picture in broad strokes—my kid attends X school and takes karate or piano or ballet. But that's about it. As for specifics—where's the karate class? what ballet school? what days do they go?—forget it!

Woody Allen was hard put to name the grades his children were in, and most men aren't much better. They don't know the teachers' names, the after-school programs, the best friends, all the details that make up a child's life. They don't know what day skirts are to be worn instead of pants, and vice versa. They couldn't tell school socks from dressy socks if their lives depended on it. They don't know who hates bananas and who won't eat their sandwiches if the crusts aren't cut off.

So you have to do the work for him. Although the temptation might be great to show how much he doesn't know and how little he's involved in their lives, for the sake of the children, you have to help him out. You don't want your kids showing up at school unprepared. It's your *kid* who won't eat if you don't warn his dad about those crusts. And your *kid* who will be hurt if she doesn't have her bathing suit on swimming-class day. I know you don't want to prop him up anymore, but do you really want your kid to miss the school trip because your husband didn't get it together in time?

One of my friends was producing a feature film in Los Angeles when she got a frantic phone call from her husband in New York. He was standing on the corner with their little girl and the bus to day camp wasn't there.

"Where's the bus?" he asked her.

Wouldn't you know he's on the wrong street? And wouldn't you know, *she* knows where he should be and she's in L.A. and he's in New York?

That's the way it goes, and you have to be there for your kids. So make things as smooth as you can for them. Send them off to your ex with an easy heart and a fully packed suitcase. If you can't bear to talk to him, write him a memo. Give him all the information he needs to know. I won't say your kids will ever thank you for being such a good guy, but you'll be doing the right thing. After all, that's what this is all about, isn't it? Your happiness and your children's happiness.

Family is everything to me. And in a time of trouble, like when your marriage falls apart, there's no one better to turn to. When women come up to me and tell me their problems, if they don't have family, if they're alone, that's one of the few times I feel stumped. I don't know how people get through a divorce without a strong support system.

On the other hand, dealing with in-laws, relatives, grandparents, best friends, and not-so-good friends can be very tricky. My parents were my best friends and my biggest boosters. They were always on my side, so I naturally assume that if you're going to have relative problems, it's going to come from your in-laws. However, I know that not everybody is as lucky as I am, and people do have problems with blood relations. In that case, you can use the same techniques I give you below. They should work just as nicely with them as they do with in-laws.

If your ex–in-laws are hostile or negative toward you there's no point in even trying to have much of a relationship with them. Since you're not likely to change them, the best thing might be if you try to have as little contact with them as possible. They'll see the children, of course, when their son has them.

If you have to talk to someone regarding the children, it's great if you can deal with a third party who's neutral, like a secretary or a nanny or a mutual friend. That way you can make whatever arrangements you need to and you don't give the in-laws a chance to provoke you.

Even if you're not on bad terms with them, you may not want to have a lot to do with your ex-husband's family. I always got along well with my in-laws. They had always been very nice to me, and I didn't want them to think I'd forgotten that. Even during that dismal period right after Aspen, when my marriage was breaking up, they were very sweet to me. My mother-in-law came to that all-girls birthday party, and my sisters-in-law did too.

I liked them and they liked me, but even so, I didn't feel like being with them much for about a year after the divorce. Of course, I sent Christmas cards and presents, and flowers on their birthdays from me and the kids, but I wouldn't call just to chat or invite them out.

This was not at all because there were bad feelings between us: there weren't. I have absolutely nothing negative to say about them—quite the opposite; they are fine people, and I believe they feel the same way about me. But I needed to separate from them in order to get over my own pain. And I believe they understood. I used to take my mother-in-law out to lunch once a month, but I stopped after the divorce. I spoke with her very honestly and openly. I said, "The grandchildren will always love you, and they will always come to spend time with you. But right now, it's very hard for me to go to lunch with you. I don't want to think about my marriage or my ex-husband. It just upsets me and I don't want to be upset. I want to forget."

So we have a kind of unspoken pact not to see each other but to think well of each other. However, I'm very aware that none of the fault lies with them. They didn't do anything wrong to my kids and my kids didn't do anything to them and I always want them to spend time together. My kids are close to their grandfather and both grandmothers. And why not? They're all good people and they adore their grandchildren.

But we don't see much of each other aside from that. You might find yourself feeling the same way. Your husband's family, much as you may like them, can't help but be powerful reminders of the life you shared with him—all the things in the past you're working to put behind you.

My mother-in-law's birthday often falls on Mother's Day, and of course we both want the children with us on that day, so we compromise. I have them all day till after lunch, say about two P.M., and then they go over to her. Or vice versa, they spend the early part of the day with her and come to me after lunch and we have a family dinner together. I don't really care which it is as long as I have them for one meal on that day.

I don't want you to be naive. Even with the best relationship in the world, you still have to know that blood is thicker than water. I think you'll be smart to expect your in-laws to take your husband's side, no matter how fond they are of you. It's only natural; he's their son, brother, uncle, or whatever.

Always remember that your kids don't divorce their grandparents. Often, if the divorce is bitter, people prohibit the children from talking to their spouse's parents,

136

and unless the grandparents have done something awful to deserve that, I think it's a shame. Grandparents are a gift, a blessing in a child's life—and my kids would be the first to say so.

Sooner or later your healing period will be over, and you will be able, and I hope ready, to start on your new life.

My husband left me feeling like I was something that belonged in the garbage can. I thought I was the most hopeless, useless, worthless person on earth. But then one day I started to think, I had a life before him. Why can't I have a life after him? I've always been somebody who likes to learn, so I focussed a lot on my job. I recently got a promotion, and now I'm in charge of my whole floor. I also went back to school and got my college degree, and now I'm working on a master's in business administration. I wake up every day with a smile on my face. And the funny part is, none of this would have happened if I was still married to him. I truly believe with all my heart that the same thing will happen to you. You may not think so while it's happening, but you'll come out of it better than you could ever dream.

Eileen

One of my friends says, "Thank God my husband was having an affair, otherwise I'd be living with him the rest of my life. I should send his mistress a thank-you note. He's her problem now, thank God."

Your healing will start the moment you truly understand that this is a new beginning. A second chance. The biggest makeover of them all. Not just a new hairstyle or new makeup; this is the makeover of your whole life!

Part 3

On Your Way to a New Life

Chapter 7

Learning New Ways to Manage Your Emotional Life

*Y*our divorce can be your license to change, an opportunity to rid yourself of old ways of doing things, things that weren't working for you, and a chance to learn new and more effective techniques for managing your life.

I think you'll find it quite liberating. It was for me; I think it can work that way for you, too.

The fact that you've been jolted out of your settled old ways is a plus, not a minus. When you were married your husband liked you to look a certain way. He expected a certain look from you. Maybe he liked beige, so you wore beige, beige, beige. You might *hate* beige. It might not even look good on you, but you wore it because you wanted to please him. He liked your hair up or he liked your hair down, so that's how you wore it. After all, for whom do we really dress? Of course, we dress for ourselves, but to a great extent we dress for the man in our lives.

Suddenly I didn't have to do that. And I changed *everything!* My hair and makeup were just the beginning. I went through my closets and weeded out all the colors I didn't like to wear but were favorites of my ex-spouse. I packed up half my wardrobe and gave it to charity. My new look was still chic; it's not that I was trying to look like a kid. But I felt younger and freer now and I wanted to reflect that in the way I looked. The very next year, I got on the best-dressed list. It's no accident that it didn't happen until I was dressing for myself, not for my husband. I felt easy and carefree and it showed. We all know that our outward appearance is ninety percent a reflection of how we feel inside.

You can weep and bemoan the past—but I hope you don't. I hope you put every ounce of energy into brightening and polishing yourself up. I can honestly say that my divorce turned out to be one of the best things that ever happened to me. I believe—no, I'm *sure*—women carry a great burden in all marriages. It's not easy no matter what your income, and not having enough money certainly makes everything harder.

The marriages I know best are in my social world, where the wife juggles the homes, the children, his work, his image, his parties, his social life. It can all grow to weigh very heavily—sometimes you're so used to it, you don't even realize it.

And suddenly it's gone. Half of your burden has vanished. It's just you and the children, that's all you have to worry about. You look good, you look happy. You look rested because you *are* rested. You can get some real rest, maybe for the first time in years. You feel taken care of because you take care of yourself. People will ask, "What happened to you, did you have a face-lift?"

You know what? You didn't need a face-lift. You needed to get rid of the stress and the worry and the burden of doing things for somebody who showed very little appreciation. Now all you have to take care of is yourself, your children, and your job. And that suddenly seems easy by comparison, because you've been doing that all along, and more.

You know what's gone from your life? Do you know what you've lost? The whining, the griping, the criticizing, and the put-downs. And I'm sure you'll miss them as little as I did. After all, things weren't great between you and your husband for some time before the breakup, and recently, they've probably been quite ghastly. Now you need deal with him very little, and only as regards the children. And if you don't have children, you never need talk to him again.

You have more time for *you*, to exercise, to have a massage, to have a facial. You can go away—just you and the kids; nobody's complaining that it's too hot, it's too cold, the plane ride is too long. Nobody's complaining about dinner arrangements that they themselves made. Some men are like a good French wine, they don't want to be moved. God forbid you take them on a trip.

You're nobody's scapegoat, nobody's whipping boy. Many men can't stand the idea of a competent woman and they do everything they can to run her down. You have to have tremendous tact to keep them from freaking out—and even then, it doesn't always work. Liz Smith once wanted to refer to me in her column as "the woman next to the man" and I said, "Please, don't get me in trouble, Liz. Say I'm the woman one step behind the man." Because I know that often men simply can't tolerate a woman's achieving as much as they—or, God forbid, a little bit more. The more successful the woman, the more troubled the marriage.

So for many women, divorce is liberating.

From what I see, maybe seventy-five percent of women are abused by their husbands in some way. The men have such big egos that they have to put down everyone else around them. Look at John McEnroe, for example. He insisted no wife of his was going to be in movies. What's wrong with being in movies? Tatum O'Neal is a wonderful actress, she won an Oscar. She's a great talent. He didn't want her to leave the kids? I'm sure she's a very good mother and she doesn't have to sit home when the kids are in nursery school. Maybe he was insecure because his career had ended, but hers hadn't. He didn't want her to be the star in the family; most men cannot tolerate this. No wonder their marriage broke up.

My friend Francesca* is good-looking and has a great personality. She runs her own public relations firm and when she's out for the evening, she bubbles and greets everyone; she's entertaining, she's fun, and she makes an effort, so naturally people gather around her. Her guy is shy, not much of a personality, and it really gets to him when everybody fusses around his wife and nobody particularly pays attention to him because he is boring! He starts to feel left out. So first he tried to keep her home. He was never willing to go out.

Finally, when she *did* manage to drag him somewhere, he'd make her life miserable. She'd get all dressed up and he'd say something like: "Do you really like that dress on you?" Francesca told me she'd feel her confidence just melt away. That sparkle that you need, that feeling of I-look-great, I'm-wonderful, I'm-going-to-have-a-great-time, would just evaporate into thin air.

That's one way to keep your wife at home, isn't it?

Men, of course, have no idea how much effort it takes for a woman to get herself turned out properly for a major social occasion. They're always making such a fuss about getting into a tuxedo. Big deal, it's pants and a blazer, a shirt and cummerbund. We have to have our hair done, our makeup, jewelry coordinated with the dress, shoes to match the dress—the handbag, God forbid it's another shade. The right pantyhose. Is it a cocktail party? Long or short dresses, fancy or casual? Is the hostess going to be in pajamas? Men jump into that suit and if they've managed to get everything zipped, they're fine. This is true universally, it seems to me, no matter what circles you travel in. The ladies get all dressed up and the guys come in jeans.

And then, after all this effort, they're at the party and someone comes over and compliments the wife: "Don't you look great!" How many times does he say, "But that color. It's not really her color"—right in front of other people?

There's no woman on earth who can stand that kind of put-down and not wilt. Another friend of mine is a world-famous designer, head of her own multimillion-dollar firm. Her husband runs the business side, and more than once I've heard her husband say to her, "Just pick the colors, honey; what do you know about finance? If I didn't make the deals you wouldn't have your 'empire.' "

But where would he be without her talent? Does he ever ask himself that? There are many business managers but very few genuine talents.

My put-down was the famous "one dollar and all the dresses I can buy." Actually, that particular item wasn't my ex-husband's fault (not that he's never put me down in his life). But this one was started by Barbara Walters, quite by accident. She was doing an interview with me at Trump's Castle in Atlantic City. I was a "dollar-a-year employee" since I didn't really need the money and I was just working for the satisfaction and fulfillment it brought me. (Later on, when I thought about it, I said, Why shouldn't I be paid? I worked hard for it. I deserve it. And ultimately I was paid a very good salary at the Plaza.) But then, for bookkeeping purposes, the finance office actually made out a check to me for one dollar at the end of the year. I had some of those checks framed on the wall in my office, and every time someone came to me for a raise, I'd point to that and say, "You won't get any sympathy from me. This is what I'm paid." I was joking, of course.

Somehow it got turned into my being paid a dollar a year plus all the dresses I could buy. It started as a fun thing, but somehow it caught the public's imagination, and people took it more seriously than it was ever intended.

> Ivana, if I were you I'd go out and buy as many dresses as you can lay your hands on.
>
> Stephanie

I'm far from the only one who found divorce liberating. My friend Cassandra* finally did something she'd wanted to do all her life. Cassie is a beautiful woman, but she had just a little too much bosom. Okay, *way* too much bosom; there *is* such a thing as too much of a good thing and Cassie was a size six in the hips and something like a 44E on top. She was very self-conscious about it—it would be hard not to be. She covered herself every way she could think of, big blazers, wraps, shawls. Naturally, her posture wasn't as good as it could have been both because of the weight of her breasts and her attempts at concealing them.

Cassandra would have had her breasts done in a minute, but her husband didn't want her to. Because he liked her the way she was? Of course not. Cassandra's husband used to tell her that her boobs were so big it was gross. But whenever she talked to him about getting a reduction he'd say, "Absolutely not." The very idea was disgusting

146

to him; it would leave her with scars, etc., etc., etc. He had a million reasons why she shouldn't do it, and with that opposition, never mind the question of paying for it, Cassandra never had it done.

Why did her husband refuse to let her have the operation? Because it kept her *insecure*—and he liked her that way. That's not unusual. I find that many husbands want their wives to be insecure—for whatever reason, some kind of sadistic or nasty instinct in them, I don't know. So they either tell their wives, "You're so stupid you can't count to ten" or find other, subtler ways to put them down. It's a way of keeping your wife under control— they think. Sometimes it works, sometimes it doesn't.

Well, when Cassandra got a divorce, you *know* she practically went straight from the courthouse to the plastic surgeon. She's still got plenty left, and she looks great, just fantastic, because now everything's in proportion.

Am I trying to imply that going through a separation and divorce is fun and games? Not at all. You won't feel wonderful all the time. You won't feel wonderful *most* of the time. I'm very aware of all the negative feelings. I've felt them all. No matter what kind of angry, vengeful thought you've had, other women have had it too. I promise.

However, thinking angry thoughts is one thing. Acting on them is another. I've cautioned you already about bad-mouthing or trying to hurt your ex in the heat of the breakup. That advice continues to apply, no matter what the provocation—and will you ever have provocation! The impulse to seek revenge, I'm sorry to say, is with you for quite a while after the split. I have no doubt that there will be many times that you will want to take revenge on your ex.

Not only will you want to, you'll *ache* to.

You'll *dream* about it.

147

You may even obsess about it.

Don't do it.

I'm saying this not because I feel for your spouse but because I feel for *you*. (Men have so many advantages in a divorce they certainly don't need my sympathy.) I don't want your focus to be on hurting him but rather on making your own life joyous and successful. I understand how angry you feel, believe me, I do. But it's a very negative use of energy, and ultimately it's pointless.

I'm trying to reason with you at a time when it's very hard for you to listen to reason. You're so hurt, so angry— you can't *think* of anything else except that son-of-a-you-know-what and how much you hate him.

But doing something nasty to him or talking publicly about what a stinker he is will not make you feel any better when you wake up the next morning.

What will? Making arrangements and plans for your new life. That's the only thing that will ultimately be of use to you, I promise. See how Paula figured that out.

For twenty-three years, I worked hard to be what he wanted me to be. Then he impregnated his secretary and the child was born while we were still married. He forced me into a separation agreement (he knew all the facts, I did not), then stopped sending me money and is trying to overturn the agreement. He has his salary, which is handsome; I have nothing. He and his "companion" are expecting a second child. He does not keep in touch with my children.

For a long time I couldn't think about anything but him. Him, him, him. Until I realized I'm not trapped; he is. He's got a tramp of a wife and two infants—at fifty-six years of age. He may think this makes him younger, but he's aging at the same rate as all the rest of us. Maybe faster, what with a wife practically his daughter's age, crying babies, and potty training.

He's trying to starve me out, but I will fight him to preserve what I can for myself and my children. And I'm going to have my revenge by leading a wonderful life, and being everything he can never be: a happy, loving, and caring human being. Ivana, they are not worth our tears.

Paula

It's very hard.

I know.

You're so angry you could beat him with your fists. But you have to let that anger go if you want to get over a bad time.

There are several things you can do to release some of this energy. One is to focus on making yourself as healthy, as attractive, and as sociable as you can, and we'll have a whole chapter on physical appearance and health later on.

But right now, I want to talk about your friends, because they can be a tremendous help to you in getting through this period.

Women sometimes ask me how they should go about notifying their friends of the separation. I don't think you should do it at all. It would be too demeaning for you to call people up and say, "Did you know my husband left me?" That's a crucifying task, and it's terrible for your ego. Don't put yourself down. The word will get out soon enough by itself. They'll find out. They'll call. They'll help you.

Not only can you complain to friends, and cry on their shoulders, you can also bounce ideas off them. I'm sure they'll stop you when you suggest following your ex in your car when he goes out on a date, but they'll also give you honest answers if you come up with ideas for your future: What if I went to hairdressing school ... or whatever? Your friends can think more clearly than you can because they're not blinded by anger. They might hate what that man did to you, but they're not crazed by it the way you are.

149

Your friends will cheer you on. What do you need him for? they'll ask you. In half a year—tops—you're going to be with somebody wonderful. You can do so much better than him, that creep!

The last thing you want at this moment is another man, but you need to hear it because you're thinking you'll never find somebody else as long as you live and if you did, he wouldn't be as good as the one you just lost. So those supportive voices countering the feelings of self-doubt and worthlessness can really make a difference.

Another nice thing about confiding in a friend or two is that you'll probably find out that they've gone through it and felt just as rotten as you do. In fact, there would be something wrong with you if you *didn't* feel terrible, given the terrible situation you're in!

I have a lot of women friends and I adore them. We have great fun together. During my marriage, my life was so terribly hectic, with flying back and forth from Atlantic City, business and social obligations, that I didn't have time to go to the girls' lunches, which is how we keep up with one another. So every year, I'd invite all my women friends to Mar-a-Lago for my famous spa weekend, which is really a glorified pajama party for grownups.

Friends would fly in from all over—Paris, Milan, London. Some socialites, some celebrities, and also my Czech friends, whom I have known from way back. I stick with my friends for life.

Some of my friends, such as Barbara Walters, Shirley Lord, and Beverly Sills, are generally recognized as being hardworking women because their achievements are highly visible to the public. But other women in my circle who don't work at paid jobs put in many long hours as volunteers for charities. (I know some of you may not believe this, but it's true.) I knew all of them were exhausted and could use a break, so this spa weekend was our time to catch up on all the pampering we hadn't had time for, and also to catch up on each other's stories.

The weekend would start Friday evening, with everyone flying in to Palm Beach after work. Of course I'd have them picked up at the airport by my car and driver.

Saturday morning we'd all take an aerobic exercise class. After that I had arranged for classes in tennis, aquatic exercise, and the like. I hired instructors, masseurs, trainers, cosmeticians, manicurists—the whole bit—to be on hand for the weekend, so anyone who wanted it could have a massage or a facial or a pedicure. But no one had to do anything she didn't want to do. There was no obligation I felt we had enough of "must do this, must be there" in real life. On this weekend, my friends could do just as they pleased—play golf, go to the beach, lounge at the pool, or participate in various activities.

Lunch was delicious but very dietetic. I would instruct my chef to prepare only very low-cal foods for the whole weekend. Later that afternoon there would be another hour-long exercise class. Then more of everything: tennis, golf, beach, whatever, followed by pedicures, manicures, and facials, all those wonderful pamperings.

In the evening, everyone would dress up—just us ladies, no men—and we'd have a formal sit-down dinner, with a strolling mariachi band for atmosphere. We'd chat and sing and just have a marvelous time.

The most wonderful thing about these weekends for me was that I helped some wonderful women become friends. At first not everybody knew everybody else, but over eight years, and eight spa weekends, we're a tight group. Women who met there have become incredible friends. I introduced Martha Kramer (head of Ungaro, USA) to Eva O'Neal from London. Now when Martha goes to London, she calls Eva and they do things together.

The whole world knew this was "women only" and respected it—except for one super-superstar. I won't name

151

him because I don't want him mad at me, but he called me because he wanted to visit Mar-a-Lago for a weekend and he picked that particular one. Actually, he called Donald first and Donald said, "I don't think she'll let you do it. Even I can't be there this weekend. Ivana has her girlfriends, and there's no men allowed."

Well, Mr. Super-superstar wasn't used to taking no for an answer. He pressed, and Donald said, "Look, call Ivana. Talk to her."

So he called me. I told him I'd love to have him at Mar-a-Lago—but not this weekend. Next weekend, fine. Any other time he wanted I'd be glad to have him.

He said, "But, Ivana, all those ladies . . . and I have such a fabulous body." I guess he thought that would make me lie down and die and give him an invitation.

I said, "You know what? So do I."

At least he laughed.

Every year while I was married I'd have a huge luncheon during the Christmas season for about eighty of my girlfriends, in their honor. We'd have it in Trump Tower or later in the Plaza Hotel. During the summer I'd have the boat moved from Atlantic City and we'd have a little cruise and a luncheon in honor of my girlfriends.

In other words, when I had this wonderful happy life, I included my friends. And when things got bad for me, they were just fantastic. I did not lose one friend. Some businesspeople, from the casino, went to the other side, and that was fine with me. But you wouldn't want people like that as friends anyway. So I didn't feel I had lost anything, and I did find out who my friends really were.

And they were wonderful.

Since my husband left me, several women who have had the same thing happen to them have been very kind to me. The ladies all loved their husbands and tried to do the best they could. I don't think it's possible to understand the hurt unless you've been through it. Some of them have financial problems and some don't, but that doesn't make any difference.

Isabelle

When I got back from that fateful trip to Aspen, everyone in the world called me, but at that time I didn't want to talk to anyone. For one thing, I couldn't. For another, I didn't want information getting out, and it does, even if the person doesn't mean it to. And then it just starts to fly around town. So for the first month or so, I didn't take any of their calls, but I did write them notes: "Dear Carolyn or Barbara or whomever, I'll call you in a little while, for now, let me just sit this out. But thank you so much for caring."

They understood a hundred percent. And then when I was finally able to see people, I couldn't leave the apartment because of all the media, so my friends came to me. We'd have tea and chat. Right away I told them that I really didn't want to say bad things about Donald (even though I certainly had some pretty bad feelings toward him at that time).

They'd hug me and let me know they would help me in any way they could. When I was able to leave the apartment, I really didn't want to. I didn't want to see people; I wanted to hide from the world and be alone with my trouble.

My friends wouldn't let me.

They'd call up—couples, husbands and their wives—and say, "Ivana, we'd like to take you for dinner." I tried to refuse, I told them I didn't feel up to socializing, but they simply wouldn't listen. "Ivana, you are going with us. We're picking you up and you're coming."

Or they'd have a party in my honor, so I'd have to go. One way or another, they'd get me out of the house and,

153

at least for a little while, talking and thinking about something other than my troubles. If they absolutely couldn't get me to leave Trump Tower, they'd call and say, "Put some champagne on ice, we're coming over—whether you want us or not."

They cheered me up enormously. They were invaluable to me. If you know a woman who's going through a separation or divorce, please do the same for her.

In general, among the people we knew, the women were on my side. They could all see that if it could happen to me, it could happen to them. They could see the unfairness, the injustice of it all. Several women I knew stood up to their husbands to defend me. Mai Hallingby went against her husband by saying good things about me and she stuck to her guns because she believed in me. And her husband had business dealings with my ex at the time! He gave her hell but she stood by me. (As I write, Mai is going through her divorce proceedings and I'm there for her all the way.)

Some of my friends were also Donald's friends and I went out of my way to make it easy and comfortable for them. I said, "You've always been my friends, I don't expect that to change because I've gotten a divorce. I don't expect you to drop my ex-husband either. I was the one who had problems with him, not you. I'm the one who's divorcing him, not you. You don't have to take sides—at least not for my sake."

I didn't lose one friend. At least not any that I wanted to keep. I did, however, ask them to do me one favor. I said I would like them to be very careful about what they said, because if I said something to them, I wouldn't like it to get back to Donald.

And even so, I was careful about what I said to them.

Be smart: Assume your friends gossip about you. They always do; everyone does. Don't be angry with them. You've probably done the same thing. If you are able to refute certain specifics, do so, but I'd suggest you try to ignore most of what's said about you. Whatever you do, don't get involved with answering every remark and challenge or you'll be slinging mud with the rest of them.

Instead focus your energies on yourself. Be happy and successful and enjoy what life has to offer. Make *your* life fabulous. It'll kill him—and you'll be so busy you won't even care. You'll stop worrying about him and his life entirely because *your* interesting life will take up all your attention. I know what I'm talking about because I was there, and I did it.

I'm reminded of a letter I got before my husband and I were divorced. This woman's circumstances were different, but she makes a good point, I think:

> Today at sixty-seven years of age I have many regrets of my younger years and decisions I made because I was a "good woman." If there is a divorce, find the courage to put yourself above Donald's interests and welfare. You have been doing this since the day you met him.
>
> Larissa

I'm proud to say that even friends and associates from my past were loyal when the press was searching for dirt on me. They naturally searched in Canada, hoping to find some good stuff there. But my friends from those years had only good things to say about me. Reporters tried the agents who handled me as a model and still got nothing. Even my ex-boyfriend stuck by me.

I can just picture how disappointed those reporters must have been. And you *know* they pushed and coaxed and tried to get people to say something "juicy" about me. They offered a lot of money in exchange for any kind of information or dirt on me. They got nothing.

At that time *New York* magazine did a cover story on me by writer Michael Gross. I didn't know him well then, but I do now. He's a friend, a decent man, but first and foremost he's a journalist. I didn't know what he would do, how he would present the story. You know, you can make something bad out of anything if you want to.

Michael called all my girlfriends—he called everybody I knew! They would immediately call me and say: "I got a phone call from this man, should I talk to him?" I said, absolutely. Because I trusted my friends. And I hadn't done anything wrong. I'm a decent human being. I didn't have to fear what those who knew me best would say. And I'd rather the people who did know me and would tell the truth spoke to Michael rather than people who just *pretended* to know me.

So my friends cooperated with him, and the story he wrote turned out very positive and protective of me.

At a time when my spirits were lowest, my friends threw me that beautiful birthday party at Le Grenouille. And when I felt worse about myself than I had in my entire life, friends of mine were instrumental in getting me on the cover of *Vogue*. I believe I was the first personality on the cover of *Vogue* who was not a model. Madonna was another. My friend Shirley Lord, beauty editor of *Vogue*, came up with the idea and took it to Anna Wintour, who approved it.

So at the most miserable time of my life, I was forced to come to life and look great. Friends gave me such a boost; they helped me to believe in myself, to remember that I had loving and supportive people around me, that I was a capable and talented woman, that I would be just fine . . . and that I didn't need "the Donald."

The smiling picture of me on the cover of *Vogue*, however much I had to force it at the time, turned out to be a prediction. The cover was shot at least three or four months before the issue came out, and by the time the magazine was on the stands, I was back out in the world, smiling.

Chapter 8

Practical Matters: Managing Your Financial Life

*M*aybe being in love means never having to say you're sorry—but I sincerely doubt it. However, being divorced almost always means you're going to have to deal with chores and responsibilities you never dealt with before.

When you were married, you probably left a whole bunch of practical matters to your husband. I'm aware that there are couples where the wife manages the finances and doles out pocket money to the man, but most often it's the other way around. As a woman on your own, you're going to have to learn to do several things you probably never did before. Isn't life interesting?

You really should start this process during the separation period. It will give you something to do and help keep you focused on that wonderful day when you will be on your own, ready to manage your money. Whether it's five thousand or five million dollars, your divorce settlement is what you have and you want to make the most of it. To do that, you'll have to learn to manage it intelligently.

I know. You've never managed money before and you have no idea how to go about it.

Look, you're going to face many tasks and do many things you've never done before. Who knew cars had to be inspected once a year? Perhaps till now you had a driver who took care of such things. I remember being stuck in Europe with a rental car and a self-serve gas station. I had no idea where the little awning is that you raise or how you unscrew that tight little thing to put the nozzle in.

Do you know what? I found out fast enough how to put gas in the car. I'm not stupid or ignorant, I just hadn't done it in fifteen years and I had to learn how. It's the same for you. If you don't know something, make yourself knowledgeable. You have done so many things in your life, you can do this too. I know that learning about finance is the last thing you feel like doing. Right now brushing your teeth seems like an insurmountable hardship!

But you have to do it. Cry when you need to, but when you're not crying, pick up the phone and make some calls.

Let's take an easy but crucial area: insurance. You need several different kinds: homeowner, car, life, boat (if you have one). Get quotes from two or three different companies. Don't worry about making a fool of yourself over the phone—they don't know you and they couldn't possibly care less.

You'll find that after the first two or three calls, you're picking up the terminology and you begin to know what they're talking about. One of the reasons I deal with insurance first is, it isn't very difficult and it's also easy to let slip from your mind. And if you don't pay, they cancel. It happened to a friend of mine. The insurance policy on her home ran out on a weekend two days after her divorce. Who knows what happened to the notice? Either they didn't send it or it was lost in all the turmoil of the divorce. Believe me, insurance was the furthest thing from her mind until she found out—by accident, mind you—that she had none. Her house was uninsured and she could easily have lost everything.

Health insurance is another area that we must deal with. You may be covered under your husband's policy or one of your own from work. If so, no problem. But please don't let yourself be uninsured as far as medical care goes. You may not be able to afford the tightest coverage, but you can get something. You don't want your illness or a child's illness to wipe you out.

Now is also the time to form a relationship with a new bank. It's a good idea to change banks, so you can make sure your banker's loyalty is to you, not to your ex, who probably has a bigger portfolio to manage. Call and ask to speak with an officer. Say that you're in the midst of your divorce but you expect a settlement of XYZ and you'd like to come in and meet with him or her personally to discuss the best way to handle your cash flow. Given the competitive situation banks are in right now, they'll be thrilled to talk to you, I promise. Whether you have a lot of money going through your account each month or not so much, go in to see them with an air of confidence. You are important. You're a customer.

If you haven't done so already, make an appointment with an accountant. If you can't afford to hire one full-time, you can meet for a consultation, just like a doctor or a hairdresser. You will pay him for his time. He might even give you the consultation for free if you say, ''I'm going to do what you tell me throughout the year and at the end of the year, you're going to handle my tax returns." Very often they'll throw in the first session since you're giving them steady business.

Again, write all your questions down beforehand and take a tape recorder. Ask the accountant to help you set up a system to keep track of your expenditures. The easiest and simplest is to have a set of envelopes or file folders, each marked with a category, such as phone, utilities, mortgage, school, entertainment . . . whatever your particular needs are. You throw your receipts inside as you get them.

At tax time you dump out the envelopes one at a time and not only do you know where everything is, you know exactly what you spent on such items as travel, vacations, clothing, and school tuition, whether deductible or not. That's a good thing to do because you'll be able to look at your spending with a critical eye. You might say, "Why did I spend so much on clothes when I really wanted a nice vacation?"—or the other way around: "Why did I take that vacation when I really needed some new clothes?" It will all become very clear to you.

Plan on seeing the accountant, say, two or three times a year if you possibly can afford it because by now you'll probably have some new questions to ask. It's a great time and energy saver.

I wouldn't let the accountant handle my funds or choose my investments for me. Get someone who does that for a living—and don't necessarily take the referral from the accountant. He or she might be perfectly honest, but they do like to give business to their friends. There's nothing necessarily wrong with that. In general, I don't mind giving business to friends rather than strangers, and you might even be getting a good rate or price because of the connection. But this friend Joe might not be the best person for you. Get a second opinion on Joe, just to make sure.

I talked with Alan Greenberg, an authority on money matters, for this book. Alan isn't nicknamed Ace for nothing. He's one of the top money men in this country. When I asked him about this, he went even further than I expected. He said, "Your accountant and your stockbroker should be unassociated. They shouldn't even know each other. The accountant should scrutinize the brokerage statements very carefully."

Make it a practice to get second opinions and to check everything—regularly, not just once a year. Things change from year to year, even from quarter to quarter and month to month. Joe-the-best-friend-of-your-accountant might be giving you a good rate this year. But next year could be a whole different story. Be vigilant. You're the driver; if you fall asleep at the wheel you have no one else to blame.

The advice I gave you about getting your entire settlement in one lump sum will work for you only if you learn to manage your money efficiently and intelligently. The responsibility rests with one person: you. You can't blame anyone else if you lose, because it's up to you to choose the right people to help you. I'm not trying to frighten you, just make you aware. There are too many horror stories of women who have been bled white by unscrupulous "investment counselors."

This money may be all you have to live on for the rest of your life. You may have to raise and educate your children with it. So as far as I'm concerned, there's no such thing as being "too careful."

So what should a woman do if she comes into a sum of money via a divorce settlement and she doesn't know very much?

I asked Ace Greenberg that question, and he said, "For one thing, she should be very careful about the stock market. She should never put money in the stock market unless she's prepared to lose it. It's like one big jungle, with

161

trap after trap to fall into. There isn't a stock I know of on the New York Stock Exchange that can't go down twenty, thirty percent in one day if a little bit of bad news comes out. IBM, Westinghouse—anytime any bad news comes out stocks react terribly badly. I don't care who she uses for a broker, there's a tremendous risk."

So why do people do it? I asked him.

"Because over time, if she uses somebody good as her adviser, she should do very well. But she's got to be prepared in the interim to see some major-league fluctuations. I say to anybody who's thinking of investing in the stock market, if you can't stand the heat, don't go in the kitchen. Because you may wake up one day and see your portfolio down really sharply in one day, and that's disquieting. The worst thing you can do is get depressed and pull out your money at the wrong time. But if you can afford to stick it out and you're dealing with quality people, you'll end up making money."

Okay, no stocks. But what should she do?

"There are basically two ways to go," Ace told me. "One is to put your money in one of the investment trusts (mutual funds). You know who the best ones are as well as I do, their records are public. There are many that have had outstanding records. Or you can entrust it to an individual whom you know, who you feel is honest and has done a good job for people."

Neither of these two is a hundred percent safe. It's not like buying government bonds or putting your money in a savings account. But then again, the returns are much greater. And as Ace pointed out, many of these funds have excellent track records; they do seem to be safe enough.

I've given you so many things to worry about, it's refreshing to have one you don't. Ace told me that brokerage accounts are insured by the FDIC and by the Securities Industry Protective Commission against theft or fraud but not against loss, obviously. He says, "When you buy stock in a mutual fund, if it's a big fund they may lose your money but it won't be due to fraud."

I'd rather not lose my money due to incompetence either, if you don't mind. So the trick now is to pick the right broker. You may feel just as insecure about picking a broker as you did about a lawyer, since chances are you've never had to do this before. In most marriages it seems the husband still handles the "big" finances. Again, you can't really evaluate the credentials or knowledge of the person you're considering. I asked Ace what he would suggest you ask a prospective broker, and his answer was: "Don't bother asking anything. If you've never dealt with a broker before, you won't know the right questions and probably won't know if you're hearing the right answers."

So how can you find a competent broker you can trust? The best way is through a friend who's had a very good experience with a broker. Not average but very good. Go for a superior reference. Otherwise, I feel you belong in a mutual fund. Ace points out: "If the broker's smart, he can come off great in the interview. We're talking bedside manner. That won't mean he truly has the means to do a great job for you. Be a results player. Use a broker who somebody you know has had a marvelous experience with. If they've had a bad experience, forget it, regardless of the personality."

Ace adds, "Tell her to be careful. There's a whole world out there waiting to steal from her. A whole world . . ."

There are so many horror stories. You read about them in the paper all the time: brokerage firms that have to reimburse clients for overtrading, for running accounts of a million dollars down to the hundreds of thousands. Trust no one. Keep tabs on everybody. Even with an honest person you have problems, so you can imagine what happens if they set out on purpose to cheat you.

Look at Gloria Vanderbilt. She apparently trusted much

of her fortune to two men who robbed her blind over the years. They overbilled, double-billed, and cheated her in more ways than you can think of. But she's guilty too, for never checking, for overtrusting, for abandoning responsibility for her money to these men. Her story was told at length in *New York* magazine, and it should be required reading for every woman.

One thing I want to warn you against, and that's investing in your brother's uncle's cousin's new business venture.

Forget it.

Just say no. If you invest, it will probably ruin your relationship with them, besides bankrupting you. At least if you invest in marketable securities and things don't go well, you can take a tax loss.

But they keep pestering you! You don't want to make them angry—you've got enough troubles with your ex-husband. How can you refuse them? It's very simple. Be honest. Say, "This is the money I'm living on. I want to buy only marketable securities, listed on the New York Stock Exchange, so if I'm wrong I can take my loss. You wouldn't want me to have to put a For Sale sign outside the house, would you?"

If you can keep your tone of voice firm but pleasant, and say this often enough, finally they'll give up. And I see no reason why they should be angry with you, although heaven knows people, relatives especially, can sometimes get upset over very little. In any case, you have to be strong.

Ace says, "I feel sorry for these women. They come into money; they have no experience, don't know where to turn, don't know what to do. Of course I'd feel sorrier for them if they didn't get the money."

Many women find themselves with less money after their divorce, and they have to let go some of the people who work for them. Given the horror stories you read in the news these days, I want to say a word about firing people, especially nannies and those who have to do with children. I don't believe you should let your nanny or baby-sitter be alone with the children after you've told them you have to let them go, particularly if the children are of preschool age.

Of course you have to be fair. You can't just dismiss someone without notice, especially if she's been with you for over six months. You'll have to pay her for the time even though she didn't actually work for you. If the nanny has been with you for two years or more, give her one month's salary in lieu of notice and a fine letter of recommendation. I'd say less than two years calls for two weeks' notice. (If you can't manage quite that much, do the best you can. You can't take food out of your children's mouths to give the nanny a parting gift. Hopefully she will understand.)

But don't let her walk out of the house pushing your baby's stroller while she might be angry or upset or disappointed in you. I hate to say it, but the kind of world we live in, people do things that you'd never dream a human being could do.

I feel responsible for the people who work for me, and in my situation, I'm able to arrange something for them rather than just firing them. When Donny, my eldest, went to boarding school, I had to take a good hard look at my nanny situation. Donny was gone; my two younger children were out of the house in school all day. After the nanny had straightened up the kids' rooms, what was she going to do? I have a housekeeper to do the cleaning and washing. While I want a nanny to be on call when the kids come home from school, in case I have to go somewhere, let's face it, I need a nanny less and less every year.

I could have let her go with a good reference, but I had a better plan. I invited her to work in my office. She took some typing and computer classes, and now she is involved in my office, preparing letters, checks, following up on paperwork, dealing with the telephone. She's basically getting a free secretarial education. If she stays with me as a secretary, great. If not, she'll be able to find a really good job and advance herself.

However, not everybody has the resources I do, and if yours are limited, I urge you to take care of your children and yourself first. I know it's hard to find a balance between caring for others and caring for yourself, but at this point in your life you have to be just a little bit selfish, for your children's sake, if not for your own. If you can't keep your staff, give them good letters of recommendation so they can move on to other jobs. All my extra help found terrific jobs after they left me because of my recommendations.

If you are a person of means, this might be a good time to hire some new staff anyway. You don't want people working for you who are loyal to your ex-husband. Remember the maid who ratted on the woman with the extra panties in her purse? Find new people whose loyalty is to you.

I've always done all my own hiring. I'll speak with somebody fifteen, twenty minutes, and I know what kind of a job they'll do and whether or not I want to hire them. By the way they answer my questions, I can see if the person is lazy or is going to have an attitude, or is ambitious and will give everything they've got to the job.

When I interview someone, I look to see if she's excited about the job. If she is, she'll give you a thousand percent. When I'm trying out a chauffeur I have him take me for a drive and then I know how he thinks, what his approach to life is. For example, when there's a traffic jam, does he sit there waiting for it to clear up or does he try to find a way around it? Tempo tells you a lot about somebody. I can tell in the first five minutes if someone is smart and quick or the opposite. You can tell a person's

energy level from the way they talk. If the person ...
speaks ... slowly ... that's ... how ... they ... work.

You can tell if someone's a wise guy—which is sometimes what you want. A bartender needs a smart line of
chatter, but the last thing I want for a waiter is a wise guy.

If the person's got ten jobs on his résumé, you know
that within half a year either he'll quit or you'll fire him.

If someone jumps from field to field, she probably
doesn't know what she wants and isn't good at anything.
If she were any good, she would have gotten offers to
stay on somewhere.

I always trust my instincts—but I also do my home
work. I don't go into a deal without checking the people
out. Once I avoided hiring someone for a deal for about
half a year; I just kept putting it off.

My assistant kept bugging me: "What's holding this
up? Why aren't we going ahead with this?" I kept saying,
"I don't have time, I can't think about it now."

In my heart I didn't want to make the deal. There was
something that bothered me about this person. I had this
little shadow of a doubt in my mind, but I couldn't express it or even put my finger on it.

I never did close the deal. Quite a long time later, I met
some people who were in the same business he was, and I
asked about him: "By the way, do you know so-and-so?"

"That crook!?" they said.

But you see, I knew that. In the back of my mind I
knew he wasn't right, that I shouldn't hire him, and fortunately I didn't.

Rana had been married to a man who knew all about
cars. He bought older, expensive cars and refurbished
them in his spare time, so during the marriage they drove
everything from a Mercedes to a Bugatti. Now she was
on her own. She bought a used car from a place where

they promised "free parts for as long as you own your car."

After a while, the muffler gave up the ghost. Rana drove her car back to the lot. They kept their promise. They handed her a muffler. Picture her standing there with a muffler in her hand and an absolutely bewildered look on her face!

Garages and auto repair shops are notorious for ripping off women who know little or nothing about the workings of an automobile. If the garage tells you you need a new screw or a new engine, you probably don't know one way or the other whether or not they're lying to you. I asked Eric, a friendly mechanic who works at M & J Auto Magic in Manhattan, if he had any advice for a woman who is faced with the upkeep of a car for the first time. He told me some of the tricks an unscrupulous mechanic might use to confuse you.

One thing they do is talk over your head. They throw a blizzard of technical words at you and the only thing you really comprehend is the number with so many zeros after it that they want you to pay them. You have no idea if it's justified or not.

You should also be suspicious if they rush you into the customers' lounge so you can't see what they're doing. If they're honest and not pulling any funny stuff, they shouldn't mind if you watch them work, as long as you're not in the way and you're not in danger. Maybe you won't understand what you're seeing but that doesn't make any difference.

What if you suspect that the garage you're dealing with is taking advantage of you? Leave. Walk out. Pay them for checking the car and take it somewhere else. And when you do find a place you like, let them take care of everything. Don't go running all over town to different places just to save a dollar or two. It doesn't pay. If you need something that they can't handle, such as bodywork, go to the place they recommend. In other words, develop a relationship with them. You won't be sorry.

Always ask the name of the mechanic who worked on your car. If the work was excellent and you go back, ask for the same man: "I'd like Carl to work on my car again." He'll know your car and he'll do an extra good job because you made him look good to his boss. Also, it's perfectly acceptable to tip the mechanic who did the work for you, and that's another way to ensure good performance. Eric says that five dollars is considered nice (more if you've had extensive work done). That way you've paid for the mechanic to go out and have a sandwich and soda; his lunch is on you—and you know he'll be happy to see you when you come back next time.

While we were chatting, Eric told me about a woman who became a mechanic after her husband died. She went to school, got her certification, and today she works as a service adviser at a large franchise in New Jersey; and all the elderly people in the area bring their cars to her. By the way, she's seventy-two.

I love this story. I wish the same for all of us, don't you? An old age filled with adventures, vigor, and achievement in new areas.

Women come up to me and say: "You have all this help and support; I'm alone with a paralyzed husband (or whatever)." I know I'm fortunate in that I have a great support system: nannies and secretaries help me organize my life. I'm grateful because the biggest problem for single parents is the lack of help. That's the one tough question that keeps coming up whenever I speak somewhere.

I tell people that I really cannot solve this problem right off, standing here, but I do know that if I were in their shoes, I would sit down and come up with a solution. I honestly believe that to be true: There's always an answer. We just have to look for it. I'm going to suggest that you sit down and think of all the possibilities you've got.

Say your husband is paralyzed. Can you arrange some kind of care for him during the day so you can work? I work with a charity for cerebral palsy patients, and many of them are picked up by bus during the day and taken to various centers where they are employed. They may have CP but they still have minds. They can write, they can talk, they can do certain functions with their hands. They can be useful and as normal as possible.

Ask your family to help you—that's what family means. They have to do it. And if they won't, or you don't have family, get a student from Europe, who will do housework or care for children or a disabled person in order to spend time in America. I had the daughter of one of my best friends in Czechoslovakia come to stay with me for a couple of months. She didn't have much money, so I paid for the crash course in English she wanted, and she helped a little in the house and with the children. When Eric was doing his ABC's, she was learning her ABC's with him. It was very charming. She went back to Czechoslovakia, and now she's a secretary in an American company there. She has a fantastic job as a secretary and a translator. Last I heard, she had met an ex-butler of mine in Amsterdam, and they're getting married! And by the way, her English is great!

You don't have to know somebody personally in Europe for this to work. There are many honorable and reliable agencies that specialize in this kind of situation. Even if you have to pay for the airplane ticket, if you get one of those supersavers, it doesn't have to cost more than a few hundred dollars.

Another way to find help is to start with local newspapers. In New York the *Irish Echo* and the *Jewish Press* classified pages have ads from people of all races and religions looking for work. Many people new to this country are desperate for jobs. If you don't want to hire foreigners, get a student. There must be a high school somewhere in your vicinity, and many of them have student employment offices where you can list a job, or bulletin boards where you can post your own notice. A sixteen- or seventeen-year-old girl can often care for a baby and get in some studying time. One of my friend's au pairs reads her schoolwork aloud to the baby as she feeds him his bottle. Let's face it, many of these girls would be doing the same work at home without getting paid for it. When the baby naps she can study all she likes—all you want to know is that your child is safe.

I'm telling you all this to prove that there's always a way. Often women look at me in disbelief when I tell them there's not just one solution to their problem—there are many solutions. But you have to think creatively, and you have to put in some hard work. The key thing is to keep from being swamped by emotion—panic or fear or depression—that won't let you think clearly. I know it's hard to do at this period of your life, but I'm afraid you'll have to manage it. There really is no other way.

Part 4

The End of the Beginning: On Your Own

Chapter 9

The Body Beautiful . . . and Healthy

*W*hen I decided that I would leave my marriage, I really started to take care of myself. Let's face it: A man doesn't need to be attractive to make a woman fall in love with him. He might be witty or funny or have all the gadgets, maybe a nice Cadillac or something like that to show off and try to get the woman's attention. But a woman needs all the femininity, sexiness, and good looks she can muster to charm a man. Hopefully the mind and personality play a role too, but we know where it starts: with the physical appearance.

I'll tell you this: It was always very clear to me what Jacqueline Kennedy saw in Aristotle Onassis. He was a dynamic, intelligent, and very sexy man. Henry Kissinger, whom no one ever accused of being a hunk, is a most attractive man—short, chubby, but quite sexy. And he happens to have a very lovely wife. Henry's brains and charm got him a woman who has brains, charm, *and* physical appeal, which I'm sure she works at keeping just like the rest of us. Who spends more time at the beauty parlor, Henry or Nancy? Who spends more time working out, Henry or Nancy? Who spends more time getting clothes fitted, face facialed, hair colored, elbows pumiced, and . . . I think I've made my point.

When my husband and I separated, I was forced to take a good hard look at myself. I made a decision: I'm never going to be older than twenty-eight. I'm kidding, but I'll give it a hell of a fight anyway. I had always been in good shape, but I got into better shape. I hired a personal trainer, purposely choosing a man. Believe me, he was gorgeous, since I hired him personally. He drove everybody at Trump Tower crazy just by walking through the lobby. I figured that if I had to do this horribly boring, repetitive stuff, at least let me have something to look at while I'm doing it. (After a few sessions, I went back to a woman because I still didn't have my divorce and I didn't want to start any rumors or be accused of cohabitation. You have to be so careful. We'll talk more about that later.) But it was nice while it lasted, and I still think it's a great idea.

I started taking better care of myself in general. Watching my diet. I had always tried to have a facial once a month, but you know how it is . . . you're busy, the facial gets lost in the shuffle. Now I made the time. I always hated the dark circles under my eyes, so I had my eyes done.

It's pretty much a sure bet that the first year after the divorce is going to be a lonely one. You still miss your ex and you probably haven't yet found a new boyfriend. However, you can put this time to good use. You were probably in no condition to make any changes in your lifestyle during your separation period. But now it's over and it's time to turn your attention to yourself.

If you're overweight, go on a weight-loss program.

Get involved with a regular exercise program.

Pay attention to your diet. Filling yourself up on sugary or fatty "comfort foods" is the worst thing you can do right now.

Rethink your whole appearance. Check out makeup and fashion trends—it's all there in the magazines. Have you been living in the fashion past? It's a trap many women, especially unhappily married women, fall into.

You don't need a lot of money to look fashionable and attractive. The designer dresses shown on the runway are copied almost immediately and sold in your local stores. All you have to do is go and look. Try on. Explore. Experiment. See? There are very nice words that start with "ex."

You know, men say they're "going on safari" when they're looking for a new girl. You really should be looking for a new man, and while I don't want to put too much emphasis on looks, that first impression is important. I do think you should try to look your best. This is a good time for a new hairstyle, new makeup, some new clothes—even have some plastic surgery if you want to and believe in it.

If you are going to start thinking of this as a beginning instead of an ending, as an opportunity instead of a tragedy, you simply have to be in good shape and feeling good. You've got your divorce and your settlement and hopefully you have a little money—what am I saying, hopefully you have a *lot* of money. But in any case, it's time to move on.

We're going to devote this chapter to the body—to getting you in shape for your new life to come. And that includes taking the very best care of your physical and mental health.

In recent years the emphasis has changed from "going on a diet" to living healthfully and eating well *all the time.* And if you haven't already made good nutrition and exercise a part of your life, I want you to make it a priority *now*. Don't tell me you don't have the time: You have to make the time! Look at the vice-president's wife, Tipper Gore, who managed to lose weight during an election campaign, a time when practically everyone gains weight due to junk food and lack of regular exercise. She stuck to her healthful practices and took off those pesky twenty-five pounds that kept her from looking like the beauty she is. She always looked sweet, but just a little too heavy. Now she's a knockout.

The point is—if you really want to do it, you'll be able to, no matter what the temptations.

Even women who don't have weight problems sometimes fall into bad food habits under stress. Whether for weight loss or simply to rid yourself of bad food habits, it can be helpful to start your new life by consulting a professional nutritionist. St. Luke's Hospital in New York City has a world-renowned Obesity Research Center. I called and spoke with Carla Wolper, a nutritionist and specialist in weight loss there, and asked her for any advice she could give. She told me that at the first meeting at the center they request a detailed medical history as well as a detailed weight history, going back to childhood: when you became overweight, if you've been overweight before at different times in your life, whether you tend to "yo-yo," that is, take off weight and put it on again. (New research shows that this can endanger your health, so if you tend to go up and down in weight considerably, maybe you *should* turn to a professional for help.)

A good nutritionist will also ask about your food preferences and eating habits so she can tailor her diet suggestions for you. Your needs will be different depending on whether you cook for yourself only, for yourself and your kids, for yourself and other family members—or don't cook at all.

She will ask at what times of the day you most feel the

need to eat. Carla Wolper told me of a patient of hers who woke up in the night, went to the kitchen, and ate. Ms. Wolper realized that it's pointless to tell this woman not to do it; if she could stop doing it, she wouldn't be in the position she's in now. Instead, Ms. Wolper divided this woman's daily caloric intake into *four* meals instead of three so that the food the woman ate in the middle of the night was incorporated in her calorie count.

My friend Kathy Keeton says, "It's not self-indulgent to take care of yourself. It's *criminal not* to!"

Kathy is superintelligent and an expert on longevity—in fact, she's president of *Longevity* magazine. We met at a press party she and her husband Bob Guccione gave about ten years ago. We liked each other on the spot, perhaps because we're both foreign-born (Kathy is a native of South Africa). But I like to think the bond between us is our humor and the loyalty we have to each other. We've been friends ever since we met, and when I was preparing this book, I asked Kathy to sit down with me and talk on the subject of taking supergood care of yourself in the Space Age. I'll tell you what she said. But just to pique your interest, let me tell you that Kathy is fifty-four (one of the down sides of promoting long life and fitness, she says, is you have to give your age), but she looks twenty years younger and is tall and blond and skinny.

Kathy says, "The most encouraging thing about women and aging is that we're seeing attitude change right before our eyes. Let me give you an example. Remember the movie *The Graduate?* Anne Bancroft played the infamous Mrs. Robinson, the 'older woman' who seduced Dustin Hoffman. Want to know how old Mrs. Robinson was? Thirty-five."

Isn't that a shocker? If they made that movie today, they'd have to make Mrs. Robinson at least ten or fifteen years older. What used to be called middle age is now thought of as extended youth, and what used to be old is now middle age.

Kathy goes on: "A woman of fifty today is young. Take a look at the female stars of today. Who's playing romantic leads? Whoopi Goldberg, Glenn Close, Susan Sarandon, Goldie Hawn, Meryl Streep, Cher, Tina Turner, Jane Fonda—the list goes on. These are all women in their thirties or forties or fifties. As recently as one generation ago, women were considered 'washed up' by that age.

"It used to be that women in Hollywood aged but men didn't. Remember a fiftyish Gary Cooper romancing a breathtaking young Audrey Hepburn—she was twenty-two or something—in *Love in the Afternoon?* That was the standard. We're lucky to be living in a time when it's changing."

Apparently researchers are still undecided as to whether having sex regularly can prolong your life, but they think it might. One way to stay young is to have lots of touching, cuddling, and sex. Anyway . . . as the joke goes, it couldn't hurt. (Provided you do it with a caring partner and take precautions.) They say that we'll see even more important and incredible breakthroughs in the next ten years. But while we're waiting for those scientific breakthroughs, we can't lose sight of two basic *proven* factors in healthy, vital, and energetic living: diet and exercise.

I personally believe you can fall off the wagon now and then and allow yourself those fattening but delicious foods. But I can do that because for me getting back on is not a problem. For some people it is, and they have to be very careful.

People often ask me how I keep my figure, and there's no secret weapon that I have that you don't, except that I was born with a certain kind of body; I'm athletic and I don't tend to put on weight. This doesn't mean that I don't watch what I eat. Who doesn't in this day and age? But I do have my own set of little tricks and rules that I follow. I know they go against what most people tell you, but they work for me.

They say breakfast should be your big meal of the day. Well, I'm not a big eater in the morning. I like that lean, mean feeling you get when you're a little bit hungry. If I ate a full breakfast like they tell you to, I'd go right back to sleep. Food makes me lose my energy. It helps that I'm a morning person anyway. At 6 A.M. my eyes spring wide open. Mornings are my best time—I get everything done then. Some people need fifteen coffees to wake up. Not me; I wake up in a good mood, instantly jump out of bed, and get on with the day.

For breakfast I have herbal tea with lemon, and often that's really it. Sometimes I'll take a slice of toasted whole grain bread and eat it plain—no butter, no jelly, perfect. Sometimes I'll have some grapefruit juice. I do worry about acids, though, and grapefruit has a lot of acid, especially if you take it by itself, so you have to be careful.

Lunch is usually pasta from the health food store and a small salad, arugula maybe, or endive. Usually there is a tomato or pesto sauce, but I don't put much on, and the portions I take are very small. I take a multivitamin with lunch along with two capsules of cod-liver oil. That's good for my back—I had a broken back from skiing and it hurts at times. I have to be careful to support it properly when I exercise.

I don't eat between meals; I don't have the time. I'm not saying that in the country I don't grab an apple or a banana, but during the week I'm too busy even to think about food.

I have a glass of wine with lunch and at about six o'clock I have another glass of wine or a cocktail. For dinner, I might have chicken or fish. I like Japanese food, sushi, sashimi—very healthy. Chinese food maybe every fourteen days or so. We all know we should drink a lot of water, but I don't like it plain. However, I drink at least ten mugs of hot herbal tea each day, which counts just the same.

When my mother is with us in Greenwich, she cooks heavy Czechoslovakian food—chicken paprika, goulash, all the pork dishes. My mother is a fabulous cook but you'd gain a hundred pounds if you ate like that. I couldn't possibly do it. You know that women in Czechoslovakia were much heavier than the ideal today, and when you see my mother's idea of a dinner table, you can see why. The kids gobble it up, but I have to watch myself.

But as I said, I do indulge occasionally. I think steak is very good for you once in a while. I have a small steak, filet mignon maybe, almost rare, with a baked potato and a salad. I like simple but good meals. Of course, sometimes I pig out like everybody else. My mother might cook a duck or for Thanksgiving a gorgeous turkey with stuffing and onions and sweet potatoes—all that yummy stuff. But the day after, I drink only tea and eat no food. In the evening, I might have a little salad. Kind of a modified fast, to balance out the day before.

I'll tell you a trick we Europeans use. If I eat something heavy, say my once-a-year duck with red cabbage, then I squeeze a whole lemon and drink the juice. I believe it helps to digest the fat. I'm not an expert, but it works for me.

I'm lucky in that I don't like sweets at all; I never did. Candy, cakes, chocolates, they just don't tempt me. Maybe once a year I'll take a piece of chocolate and immediately break out. Who needs it? But I do love cheeses and pâtés. In America, the pâtés are okay but not great so it's easier to resist them than it is in France, where they are just sublime. I save my pâté and terrine calories for France. In Italy I indulge my craving for cheeses. Fresh mozzarella, yum.

I believe cheese is okay as a last course after dinner,

and you can have a chocolate mint if you want, but as far as I'm concerned, fruit is the worst thing. It is the practice to serve fruit after dinner almost everywhere you go, and I know the experts tell us to have fresh fruit for dessert, but it doesn't agree with me. The combination of acids and sugar really messes up my digestion. (The lemon juice at least has no sugar.) When I used to eat fruit last thing after dinner, it took me the whole night to digest it, so I leave it alone.

Somebody once told me: "Ivana, when you're about to sit down to order a meal, imagine them putting each thing you order in the blender with all the others." It's a ghastly thought: salad, duck, red cabbage, and whatever else the duck is served with, then dessert, and on top of that acidy fruits, oranges, grapes—horrible. But salad, fish, and potatoes or rice doesn't seem like such a disgusting mess. It's a cute little trick and I use it.

My boys like steaks and hamburgers, especially on the grill. And french fries—kids do love french fries. As long as my kids are slim and healthy I have no problem with their eating foods like that occasionally. For the most part I like them to eat fish, chicken, vegetables and fruits, and lots of pasta, which they love. They also adore pizza, so I might get a pie for them on weekends, and I might have a slice along with them or perhaps I will have sushi or sashimi or grilled fresh fish. I love sushi, but the kids are not that crazy about it. For lunch I might do pasta with meatballs for them, but I might have the pasta plain, or just with some tomato sauce. Let's face it, the kids seem to burn up all those calories, but we adults just can't eat like that anymore. The metabolism of a teenage boy is amazing. Just double every recipe for each of them. Ivanka is more like me. She likes baked potatoes and fish.

I read that people who exercise regularly get fifty percent fewer colds, flus, and viruses and recover fifty percent faster, and I believe it. I exercise every day and I'm never sick. I don't know where the Tylenol is in my house, and we wouldn't have it at all if it weren't for guests and staff.

I've worked out all my life—even when I was pregnant, until about the seventh month; then I took it easier. But even then, I did a lot of walking and stretching. I'm lucky in that I don't have a specific problem area to worry about. Some ladies have to work on their butt or tummy for hours. I do general maintenance, working out about an hour a day, three times a week, on Monday, Wednesday, and Friday. Over the weekend I'm in the country and I garden, water-ski, play tennis, hike, walk a lot, so I don't work out unless I've had to go for three or four days without exercising, say, if I've been on a book tour. In that case, I have a session on the weekend to make up. I do try to make that three-times-a-week workout happen.

As you could probably guess, my workout time is early in the morning. Before my trainer comes, I do ten minutes on the bike to warm up and get my heart rate up. When the trainer comes in, we do aerobics for about ten minutes, because you really need to do the full twenty minutes of aerobic exercise to get the benefit and burn calories. By then, I've had enough jumping up and down; I'm not training for a marathon, I just want my heart and circulation to be healthy. Five minutes of stretching—very important—then I immediately get on the floor, and I do as much as I can on my stomach and butt before turning over on my side to do the leg work. Then I do push-ups and sit-ups and a little bit with weights for the upper body. Some pelvic tucks lying flat on my back, some abs work, and I end with about five minutes of real stretching. Some people work out for two or three hours a day or more—Cher is an example—but I think a body can take only a certain amount of "abuse." Besides, I don't have the time.

There's no excuse to stop your workout when you travel. All you really need are a towel and the floor. And there are always the stairs, a marvelous invention. I try to walk both up and down stairs, if it's at all possible. Even when I lived in Trump Tower, on the sixty-seventh floor, if the trainer didn't come, I would walk down to the thirtieth floor and then walk up thirty-seven floors. Or I'd take an elevator all the way down, and try to walk up sixty-seven floors. It's a great exercise.

I even did it when I was four months pregnant. There was a famous blackout—I was carrying Donny, so it had to be 1977. Donald was away on a business trip and when the blackout struck, I drove across the bridge to New Jersey because I knew there was no blackout there. I stayed in a New Jersey hotel close to New York City, and then in the morning, I had to come back to the city because my dog was alone in the apartment. At the time we were living on the forty-ninth floor of Olympic Towers.

Nobody else would do it, so I did. I walked up the stairs and rescued my dog. Nobody wanted me to do it, but nobody else would. (I should say that at the time, Olympic Towers was brand new and only partially rented and staffed.) I knew I could do it, no big deal, but it was very hot inside the stairwell. When I got up to my apartment, I was soaked with sweat and of course the water wasn't running. Fortunately I always have a few gallons of bottled water on hand. I stood in the bathtub and poured Evian over myself, changed my clothes, got the dog, walked down forty-nine flights, and drove to East Hampton, where we had a summer cottage.

When I travel I do fifty push-ups and fifty sit-ups in the morning, and fifty in the evening—a hundred every day. You burn off so much shlepping from one airport terminal to another, you really don't need to exercise as much, but you still want to keep your tummy flat and work your arms and upper body.

If you can afford one, a personal trainer is wonderful. However, as with everything else, I believe you should get someone who knows what he's doing. That's why I spoke with Dr. Michael Ross who has a Ph.D. in sports psychology and owns a health club in Manhattan called Aerobics West.

Dr. Ross recommends that if you are seriously out of shape—or even if you're not—you should check with a physician before you begin a workout regimen. Then check out your local health clubs. First notice the environment of the club. Some clubs cater to the "hot body syndrome," others are more low-key and informal.

"You could hire a trainer just to set you up with a program, if you're motivated enough to carry through on your own. Then you can bring him in once every few weeks to make sure you're doing everything right and to make any changes that are needed in your program. The people who need a full-time trainer are the ones who are not motivated, who want to be hand-held.

"Of course the single biggest factor is the commitment the person makes to themselves. How you will look is affected in part by genetics. If you have a predisposition to carry a lot of fat on your bottom, with a good exercise-diet program you can keep it within reason as opposed to letting it go unchecked.

"If you sign up for a series, ask if they give a discount. Also, you can link up with a friend. Many trainers will give discounts for two people who take a class simultaneously. Basically it's up to you. We've got the pool; we can't make you swim laps. We've got the equipment; you have to do the workout."

Many people who can't afford a personal trainer *can* afford a gym membership. And if that's still too expensive, or the gym isn't practical for you, there are many

186

marvelous exercise videos on the market. They seem to have one to suit just about every taste, and it's not a big splurge to treat yourself to a new one when you get bored with the one you have. It's a good idea to have several and change off anyway, if you can, because it's important to vary your routine. Otherwise your muscles easily get used to a certain routine and you don't progress as much as you should.

Many public libraries will also rent videotapes and you can try them out before you buy. I'm leaving you almost no excuses, aren't I? Walking is free and so are stair climbing, sit-ups, and push-ups. So money isn't much of a factor in whether we work out or not, right? Of course a personal trainer makes it more pleasant, but if you want to . . . you can. That's all.

If your kids give you a hard time when you try to do your workout, why not get them exercising with you? This may not work for everyone, but if it does work, it's a terrific idea. You spend time together, get strong and healthy and stress free as a family. I exercise with Ivanka very often.

Diet and exercise may or may not extend your life, but they can improve the *quality* of your life. Who wants to be alive and kicking if you're in bad shape and feel worse? You want to feel good and look good for as long as you can.

As I told you, I myself have decided to be no older than twenty-eight—in my mind, anyway. I encourage you to make the same decision. We'll stay young together. Why not?

I've noticed that very often women who are divorcing or leaving a marriage finally have the plastic surgery they've been thinking about for a while—and I say, why not? When I started writing this book, I called my friend Steve in Los Angeles—the plastic surgeon I sent Natalie to—and asked him if he would mind sharing with us some advice for a women in her forties or fifties, let's say, who's considering plastic surgery. I'm going to pass on to you what he said. (For the record, he's Dr. Stephen Hoefflin, M.D., F.A.C.S., which stands for Fellow of the American College of Surgeons.)

First of all, he told me that plastic surgery is very popular. (The ratio is about four or five women to one man.) Having one's eyelids done is common. So is skin care (chemical peeling), because there are so many new techniques available to improve the color and texture of the skin. (A chemical peel doesn't take care of loose skin. For that you need a face-lift.) The newer techniques for chemical peels involve the use of Retin-A, antioxidants, and glycolic acid. You might want to mention these three things to your plastic surgeon if you're interested in exploring them.

(While we're on the subject of skin care, many women today are using products made with Retin-A to slow the aging process. But to me that's passé. I'm excited about a much gentler substance made from natural products like sugarcane and fruits, which I believe is much more healthful and less drastic than Retin-A. It is called alphahydroxy acid and my new Ivana line of cosmetics will be based on it. Let's postpone surgery as long as we can by taking good care of our skin beforehand, and also afterward.)

I didn't mean to interrupt. Back to Steve. One thing Steve told me absolutely fascinated me. Apparently they can take fatty tissue from elsewhere and use it to enlarge the cheekbones. I call that the best use of body fat I ever heard of! The idea of recycling fat from your fanny to your cheekbones strikes me as incredibly clever. How many times have you said you wish you had more boobs and less hips or more cheekbones and less thigh? You might just be able to, if you have a talk with your friendly plastic surgeon. Cheekbones can also be enlarged by using cheek implants or fat injections, but the latter may not last long, according to what Steve told me. Fat injections are also used around the mouth to get rid of those little lines that make a woman look so crabby, or to make the lips themselves larger and more luscious. However, these procedures have to be redone every six months or so; it's not a one-time deal.

The most popular surgery with men, by the way, is eyelid lift, followed by face-lift, nasal surgery, and lipo-suction. For women, in order of popularity, it's face and eye lifts, nasal surgery, chemical peels, forehead lifts, lipo-suction, and breast reduction. I suppose none of them needs much explanation. The forehead lift improves the position of the eyebrows, which tend to drop with age, and helps to alleviate frown lines. Liposuction is a way of removing fat directly from the abdomen, waist, thighs, or hips. On some people, nothing else will work—not di-eting, not exercise. For them, liposuction might be the only way to get rid of a stretched-out abdomen or chunky, out-of-proportion thighs or bottom.

One of the things Dr. Hoefflin was very adamant about is that prospective patients take an active and intelligent role in their surgery. How do you do that? First of all, by choosing your doctor very carefully. Steve points out that people often put more effort into researching the purchase of a car than the selection of a plastic surgeon. Plastic surgery is an operation, a medical procedure, and you should approach it with care, don't you think? It's very important that you do your homework before having any work done on yourself.

I know you are probably thinking right now that you know less about choosing a plastic surgeon than you did about choosing a divorce lawyer or a money manager. Well, I'm going to help you. There are three areas you should look into. You have to investigate the surgeon, the procedure, and the facility.

Let's take the surgeon first. The simplest way to find

someone is through people you know who've had good results from their surgery. However, more plastic surgery is done than is talked about; you may not even know who's had what done. Also, you may not wish to announce your surgery to anyone. That's no problem. You can call the American Society of Plastic and Reconstructive Surgery, at 800-635-0635, and they will give you the names of qualified doctors practicing in your area.

If someone gives you the name of a surgeon and you want to check out his qualifications, it's very easy to do. Go to a medical library, which you will find at any hospital in your area, and consult the *Directory of Medical Specialties*.

The next step is making an appointment for a consultation, in which you explain to the doctor what you are interested in improving and listen to his suggestions. Dr. Hoefflin won't take on patients who seem to have unrealistic expectations. His goal is a natural but more attractive appearance. He can't turn you into a completely different person: You won't look like Michelle Pfeiffer unless you are Michelle Pfeiffer. But you can look as good as you can look.

I have a friend who had a not very nice nose. Let's face it: It looked like a potato. But she lived with it and it was part of her charm—and don't misunderstand me, her charm was considerable. Ruth was fifty when she decided she'd seen that nose on her face once too often. She flew to Florida on "vacation" and had her nose done.

Do you know what? Nobody noticed. The surgeon made her nose smaller, narrower, and took the bumps out. But it still looks like her nose. It belongs on her face. That's good plastic surgery. Everyone tells her how good she's looking lately; that vacation did wonders for her. (I know about it only because she confided in me.) Ruth smiles to herself as she takes in their compliments. Yes, that Florida vacation was long overdue. It made a new woman out of her.

Anyway, Dr. Hoefflin won't take you if he feels you're

being unrealistic. Or if you're not in good health, mentally and physically, or if you're under a really tremendous amount of stress, since such people often don't heal as well. At times he will suggest that people postpone the surgery and get into better shape before he'll operate on them.

Dr. Hoefflin spends a great deal of time preparing the patient, making sure she understands the surgery and what he hopes to achieve with it. The doctor should be honest with you about the possible risks of the surgery, without frightening you unnecessarily. Yes, it's a real operation. However, it's very, very rare that somebody dies from plastic surgery. Think about it: The biggest risk you take in life is when you get into a car. But nonetheless the doctor should discuss the risks with you at length.

In selecting a plastic surgeon, ask him if he has often performed the procedure you are contemplating.

Then ask yourself how you feel about him after your consultation. Needless to say, you should feel comfortable.

You can ask to see samples of the doctor's work. He may show you photos, or put you in touch with actual patients of his. After all, you wouldn't hire a contractor to put in a new bathroom without seeing examples of his work, would you?

The next area you should investigate is the procedure itself. Dr. Hoefflin feels you should know about it in detail. I'm not sure about this. Some of the things they do seem quite scary when you read about them. If somebody's going to pull the skin off my face and put it back when they're done, I'm not sure I want to know about it. However, your doctor should give you plenty of literature on the procedure, and Steve also suggests you look it up in a medical library.

Much plastic surgery is done on an outpatient basis in a hospital or in an operating room in the doctor's office.

However, many people do spend a night either in the hospital or in a recovery center. Recovery centers are the newest wrinkle (excuse me!) in this kind of surgery and they're very popular. You have the procedure in the doctor's-office operating room, and after you wake up they put you in a limo and drive you to a luxurious place staffed with nurses, where you can spend the night. It costs less than a hospital, and you really don't need a full-scale medical center. What you need is a lot of pampering, and that you'll get.

I asked about pain. The good news, Steve says, is that there isn't much. He uses a long-acting local anesthetic plus plenty of sedation. If the patient prefers it and if the procedure warrants it, he will use a general anesthetic. Most people undergoing something substantial, he says, want to be out cold.

Whether your surgery is done in a hospital or a doctor's office, make sure the facility is approved and accredited. That's the third area you need to investigate before having surgery.

Generally, the stitches start coming out a few days after surgery and they're all out two weeks later. Most people can go out in public at that point, but it may take four to six weeks before you feel fully returned to yourself.

As we said, there are risks. But Dr. Hoefflin feels they can be reduced if the patient participates actively, chooses a surgeon well, and then follows the surgeon's instructions as exactly as possible.

My feeling about all this is, if you can afford it and if you want it, go ahead. Why not? I'm in favor of anything that makes you feel better, gives you confidence, and improves your image of yourself—especially at this time in your life when you're feeling awkward and uncomfortable socially anyway.

Chapter 10

Yes, You'll Have a Social Life!

*N*ewly divorced—no, newly *single*—women are often terrified of going anywhere because they're afraid they'll run into *him!* And even worse—what if they run into him and he's got a NEW GIRLFRIEND!!!?

My attitude is, if it happens, it happens. Chances are you're going to keep going to the same restaurants and so is he. What are you going to do, turn on your heel and leave? I'm too proud for that, and I hope you are too. It's undignified, and I wouldn't give him the satisfaction. You have as much right to enjoy the restaurant as he does and you're not going to let him drive you out of places you enjoy.

Don't make a scene; you'd only be making a fool of yourself and embarrassing your friends. Ask for a table away from them, so you don't have to stare at each other over the soup. You won't enjoy your dinner if he's sitting right next to you.

Keep thinking: This man has ruined so many evenings for me. Am I going to let him ruin one more? Sit on the other side of the room, and enjoy your dinner.

If it's a private party, your hostess should warn you if He's invited too. If for some reason she didn't do that and you're taken by surprise, you can go to the hostess quietly and explain that you don't feel comfortable, you'll see her another time. And then just leave.

But if you can stand to do it, I think you should stay and ignore him.

If you're easily fazed and distressed socially, I think you have to work at developing a thicker skin. Fear of embarrassment can be so paralyzing. The one sure way never to take an ungraceful step in public is never to leave your home. But what kind of a life is that? We all have moments of feeling self-conscious and shy—but I say, the fewer the better. And if it's a problem for you, you have to consciously train yourself to ignore those moments or you're going to miss out on a lot of fun.

However, what *is* difficult socially, I admit, is being without a "significant other." I hate dining alone, and when I travel on business, if I don't have my assistant with me, I eat in my room. But I'm in a different situation than most people. If I sat at a table by myself, I would be the evening's entertainment! They stare even if I'm with someone, of course, but if I'm talking to my companion, I'm not so aware of it.

Sometimes I'm in a fine restaurant or at the opera or other social event and I see a woman out for the evening alone, and I honestly don't know how she does it. For a man it is acceptable somehow, but a woman dining alone—I feel sorry for her. I think, maybe she just doesn't have somebody she will enjoy spending the evening with. But can't you always get somebody to join you?

Husbands are handy—they're a permanent, on-call escort, if you will—and when I no longer had one, I had to figure out different ways to cope, and I think you can adapt many of them for yourself.

The most comfortable situation is one I control, like charity balls. I'm not suggesting that I think you'll be spending a hundred thousand dollars on a table at a charity benefit, but you can think about what I do and I'm sure you'll find a way to make it work for you. The point is, I'm the one who set up the evening, so I have the reins in my hand. Let's say, for example, that I've taken my own table for a charity evening, I don't want to meet my guests at the ball, because then I'll have to arrive alone, so I have my friends join me at home where we have our drinks and then we all go on to the ball together.

If I'm invited to join somebody else's table, usually the hostess will call and ask how I'm getting there and if I want to be picked up. If she doesn't, I phone her and suggest we go together; there's nothing wrong with that. People will be happy to accommodate you, and this holds true no matter where you plan to go, a party, a movie, whatever.

Once you've arrived at the party, you're fine. Think about it; even when you come with an escort, people mingle. Sometimes your date is talking over there while you are here, and you don't get together again until you go to the table for dinner. So if you don't have a partner, you won't even notice the lack. (If it's a movie or bowling or something, even better.)

At the table, you have an assigned place. You don't lack for conversation or dance partners because the hostess has seated you man, woman, man, woman, so you have a man on either side. You can converse all evening, and they'll take you out on the dance floor.

At the end of the evening, you can usually move toward the door with other people so you're not a lone woman leaving by herself. Often I'd go out with a couple and we'd walk in wherever we were going as a threesome. Larger groups of five, six, or seven are even better since they don't tend to break down into couples in the same way. You don't feel you're "extra" and you have no pressure to scrounge around for a warm body to fill that space.

How difficult it will be to go out without an escort depends on where you're going. At a friend's house I feel perfectly comfortable dining without an escort. But you can't go to the opening of the ballet season alone. If you're dining in a restaurant, you can just walk in alone and join the group; that's easy enough. But if you're going to the Plaza Hotel for a beautiful black-tie dinner, pulling up alone in a taxi just doesn't feel right. Especially in my case, since I'm greeted by photographers on arrival. And walking into a ballroom by yourself instead of on a man's arm—it's not unacceptable, but it is awkward.

Even though you know better, you think everyone is saying: "Poor her, she can't get a man." Reminding yourself that at this minute you don't want a man doesn't help all that much; it still doesn't look right for a woman to be out on her own. You need someone to enter the room with, someone to take your wrap, to take care of you, bring you a drink, all the little social attentions. It helps you enjoy the evening.

Society has a marvelous invention for women who for one reason or another are not romantically linked and don't want to appear to be. Certain friends—and everyone knows who they are—are accepted as escorts and escorts only. It's like a code that everyone knows. If you're out with them it's just a friendly evening; purely social, no romance involved, and everyone knows it. (I personally don't think of them as "walkers." They are my very good friends.) Nancy Reagan favored Jerome Zipkin whenever

Ronnie couldn't or wouldn't go out with her, and I can see why. Jerome is marvelous company, very entertaining, and he knows everybody. When I say he knows everybody, I mean he really knows them. Point out a lady and he knows about her family, going back five generations. He knows about culture and art—a charming escort for an evening.

Another man I love to spend an evening with is Kenneth J. Lane. He's one of my best friends—funny and intelligent and altogether delightful. I found these friends very comforting in the months after my divorce. No pressure: You enjoy the event, the ballet, the opera, the ball, whatever; they escort you safely back home like the gentlemen they are, no kootchie-kootchie, no making a pass. A kiss on the cheek, a "thank you for a marvelous evening," and everybody is happy.

When you first start to socialize after your divorce you'll probably feel awkward no matter what arrangements you make. But don't fall into the trap of allowing your discomfort to keep you at home. You have to get out and see people, even if you must force yourself to do it. Looking at the four walls with only memories for company would drive anyone crazy.

A good place to start going out is church; you meet nice people there. If going to concerts, movies, ballets, lectures, museums, exhibitions, and the like by yourself makes you uncomfortable, take a girlfriend. If she can't afford it and you can, treat her. This is a time for you to be very good to yourself. And if you're not in the habit of indulging yourself with small luxuries, this is a wonderful time to start.

You can't avoid loneliness altogether that first year, I don't think, but you can make it easier on yourself by planning ahead. I suggest you think in terms of one full year, let's say from September to September. Using the school year comes naturally if you have children. Think of this as intensive recuperation time.

Now—look at the calendar and plan that year out in detail. Start with major holidays. Usually they're divided up between you and your ex-husband so that he has Christmas Eve one year and Christmas Day the next, or vice versa.

If you have the kids, fine. If not, arrange to do something that you'll enjoy. But *arrange it in advance*. Don't leave it up to chance. Have something firm locked in. Theater or concert tickets are a great idea and, you know, excellent seats are usually available on holidays.

Invite someone over or go to their house. Many women feel more secure on their home ground, which is perfectly understandable. (I adore entertaining but I also adore being entertained.) It's natural for you, when you're just divorced (I'd rather call it newly single, which refers to your current state as opposed to something that happened to you) to feel a little shy or awkward when you start seeing people on your own, without your old familiar hubby at your side.

Whatever you do, I urge you to make plans for holidays, so you don't find yourself all alone on Thanksgiving morning feeling terribly lonely and crying your eyes out only to have your friends call you after lunch saying if only they knew you were alone you could have come and eaten with them. Of course they beg you to come over now, but you've already lost the morning you spent crying, your head hurts, and you feel just awful, so you refuse.

There's nothing worse than finding yourself staring down at a holiday meal on your wedding china, service for one. Don't let that happen to you. It's completely avoidable if you plan ahead. You know there will be a time when the father has the children full-time. This might be over Christmas vacation or summer vacation. Leaving yourself at loose ends is a good way to sink into depression.

If you want to make a small party, I have a fail-safe way for you to do it that will work winter or summer, Christmas or Fourth of July. Whenever I serve my famous blini, everyone winds up having so much fun filling the little crepes with the variety of toppings I set out that no one has any time to be awkward or shy. People are always the least self-conscious when they have something to focus on other than themselves, and standing before an array of toppings is a natural conversation starter.

One caution: Do not make this a sit-down dinner! Do it buffet style The fun is to keep everybody circling around, seeing what there is, trying things, and making their own combinations. That's the charm of my blini with fillings—and it's a main course *and* dessert too. Could you ask for anything more? If you wish, of course you can have it with only savory fillings and have something else for dessert, or you can have a dessert-only party, which is a lot of fun.

Teenagers will love it too, so if your youngster needs a boost socially, throw a blini party. The recipe does take some work, but you can do it ahead of time. If you don't know how to make blini, ask a friend or look up a recipe in a cookbook.

Once you have the crepes, you can get creative with the fillings; they can be savory or sweet. For savory, try caviar, sour cream, chopped onion, chopped hard-cooked egg, salmon flaked in a mayo-yogurt-dill dressing. For sweet, make instant vanilla pudding with half the milk recommended on the box and add two tablespoons of a fruit-flavored liqueur, mixed with one cup of freshly whipped cream. This mixture can be used alone or with any of the following: fruit preserves; fresh berries and whipped cream; fresh peaches or pineapple cooked with

Grand Marnier or other fruit-flavored liqueur; chocolate sauce, whipped cream, and a sprinkle of cinnamon.

Tell me the truth: Doesn't it put you in a good mood just to *think* about throwing a blini party?

During the separation period, women are often afraid to leave town for any length of time. The battle between you and your husband is raging, so you don't want to lose contact with the lawyers. If you feel this way and you want to stick to just weekend vacations, there's nothing like a spa. I would venture that every place in the country is within a short flight to one spa or another. You can go on Thursday morning and come back Sunday night; three days and you feel like new.

The Grand Canyon Ranch, the Miami Doral, or the Golden Door in California seem to be the most popular. You're with other ladies who might be in the same situation, that is, alone, so you don't feel out of place. You exercise, get massaged, manicured, and pedicured. You're being pampered, and even though they barely give you one carrot a day to eat, you'll find you have great energy. I believe that every woman who can afford it should go to a spa once or twice a year. You become so rejuvenated and feel healthy and full of vigor when you come home. If it's outside your budget, perhaps you can go just this once, on the first holiday season after your divorce (or separation). If you can manage it, do try, because I promise you won't feel lonely or sorry for yourself while you're there.

Cruises are another option. I myself have never been on a cruise ship. I either had my yacht or friends' yachts, but I often hear from ladies who have taken cruises and they seem to have enjoyed them very much. If you can afford it, you might want to try one.

On a cruise, the ship docks someplace beautiful; it's sunny and the air smells wonderful. There's a magnificent beach or interesting town to explore. You go sightseeing, you talk to new people, and you get your mind off what's going on at home.

You might want to avoid going to romantic places or to places where you went with him. If the Bahamas or Hawaii are out, go to Alaska instead. How many people do you know who've seen the Northern Lights? Or take a safari. Maybe you'll discover you're an animal lover.

Christmas Eve in Vienna is fabulous.

If you can't afford spas or cruises, no matter where you live, I'm sure there are interesting and scenic places to visit within a day's drive or train trip. You always meant to go—now's your chance.

Going anywhere is better than sitting home alone. It's a different scene, different people; you have an incentive to go out in the evening, if only to sample an unfamiliar type of cuisine. In order to go out to dinner, you have to do something with your hair and put on makeup. It helps you to feel like your old self.

You can't go away for every holiday—your finances won't allow it—but you *can* plan for every holiday. And by the way, if you don't have children, or they won't be with you, think of devoting some time to charitable operations. There are groups that prepare and serve dinners to the homeless or needy at Christmas and Thanksgiving. You'll be among people, you'll be doing something useful—and you're going to have fun, I promise you. How can you be depressed with people and food and laughter all around you?

I'm trying to get you to think creatively and with a zest for life instead of sinking into despair and depression.

There's always an answer. When you feel despairing, remember Ivana told you that.

Chapter 11

Romance after Divorce? Of Course!

*B*efore your divorce was final, you didn't feel like being with a man in a "date" situation. I know I didn't. Also, you're afraid it's going to hurt you in the divorce settlement—and it definitely can. Sure, you can go out to dinner with a man, but you should expect your soon-to-be-ex to act like you just kidnapped the Lindbergh baby. Exes get extremely jealous and possessive: "If she's going out with another man, let him pay for her."

But the day comes when you go out and buy a whole bunch of gorgeous new lingerie. You get rid of your grungy married-woman's underwear and go for the colors and the silks and the lace. I got tons of panties and lacy bits in all colors to help me get over the feeling of being undesirable and unwanted, which is practically a certainty at this point.

Suddenly, you *want* to look sexy and desirable. You

start to flirt again, although you practically have to relearn how to do it since with your husband, flirting wore off years ago. Learning to flirt is just like learning to cook. You probably know how, all you need is a little practice. You'll remember soon enough how to be the coquette without overdoing it; how to keep eye contact, stare at a man, look away, stare again.

A touch on the knee can be a very nice gesture, but if you do it at the wrong moment, you can look like you're making the moves on somebody when you're not. I tend to be a toucher, but it has no significance and I have to be careful so I don't give people the wrong idea. A young reporter once wrote, "I got the biggest thrill, Ivana flirted with me—she touched my knee!"

> I'd been divorced a year when I started going out again. It still felt like I was committing adultery.
>
> Vivian

Chances are you've completely forgotten how to date! You've forgotten what to say, what to do, how to negotiate that whole awful scene: "Where are you from, what are your hobbies?"

I'm not saying a blind date can't be exciting. It can. But if your face falls into the plate because you're bored to tears, there's not much you can do but pray for the dinner to be over. You know what they say: You have to kiss many frogs before you find a prince.

How is your ex going to feel about the fact that you are now dating? Darling, we don't care. Unless there's something he can do to bother or distress you. We are going to pay attention to our own lives, remember?

As a newly single woman, you have to be careful. There are two dangers: giving your heart too easily, and being so locked in on yourself that you don't let yourself get close to a new man. You're very vulnerable at this time in your life. Your emotions are up and down and left and right—all over the place. You feel like a failure and your confidence as a woman is zero.

You've been through hell.

You're likely to fall for the first man who comes around and is nice to you. He opens the door, brings you a shawl—the little things that show that he cares, that he has you on his mind.

You miss that kind of attention; it's been gone from your life for so long—long before your divorce. I'm sure if you mentioned to your husband that you had a little headache, he said he did too. But this new man runs for the Tylenol. He showers you with attentions, those small gestures that mean so much. He sends flowers—and by the way, that's how you'll know when you've reached the real courting stage—when he starts sending flowers.

It's lovely. You feel something in you that you feared was dead come to life. But the question is, are you falling in love with *being loved* or with the person?

Beware of thinking you're in love when it's really the *idea* that somebody enjoys you, likes your company, finds you beautiful, attractive, sexy, witty. Because it's intoxicating. Especially now, when you've been made to feel for so long that you're about as attractive as yesterday's dinner. Your ex-husband humiliated you and belittled you and probably still does . . . and here's a man who's crazy about you.

Women tell me, "I was treated so badly by my ex that when someone was the least little bit nice to me, I fell in love." And that's the danger. You have to be careful that you're falling in love with an actual person, not with how much he's willing to love you and pamper you.

The other pitfall is that you've been burned and now you're afraid of the fire. You tremble at the thought of being dumped again. Another rejection would be more than you could take, so you stop yourself from responding to the new man. And of course, no one likes to flirt with a mannequin. If you don't let your heart beat faster, he'll move on, and who can blame him?

The only answer is time. It takes a while to get over that feeling—and as a matter of fact, you never do completely. I still feel that way. I'm very aware of myself with men, consciously watching myself in a way I didn't before. I think it will take me ten years to recover, and I may never be as trusting as I was. I don't think I'll ever let down my guard as completely as I once did. Now you look at a man and you say, God forbid something like that should happen to me again. You have some kind of internal reaction, you close up inside. It's almost like you're giving up on relationships with men, on this institution called marriage. But you cannot allow this to happen because you won't be able to start a new relationship without trust.

So you have a real conflict. You want to get into a relationship, but in the back of your mind you have this terrible awareness of what happened to you. All the while you're listening to your new man swear he loves you and he'll die without you, you remember how your ex told you the same thing.

And you can't hear a word your beau is saying: The sound of promises breaking is deafening you. The new man adores you. He cherishes you. He whispers words of love. And you're wondering, if you marry him, will he sue you one day for all you've got? One thing you promise yourself: You don't ever again want to go through another divorce, another division of property, another series of lawsuits and settlements.

Sometimes you even think you've gotten past it. You're productive; you do well at work; the divorce is behind you.

But it's not. It's still there; buried deep, but there.

You're a little more wary than you once were. A little more suspicious. You question motives; you hold back from giving your feelings and your heart. We women are different from men; we give our hearts completely. We fall for a guy, and we're his. We're emotional, yes. But we have to learn to think.

I suppose it's sad to lose that innocence, that sense of trust in people. But it can't be helped and you do have to protect yourself, especially if you've come out of a divorce with a sizable settlement. You have to be very careful who you go out with.

Some women after a divorce choose not to date at all. They close themselves away with their memories and their pain. That's their choice, but I don't think it's the best one. If you want to make something of your life, you have to open yourself up to others, even knowing up front, as you do now, that the possibility exists that you will be hurt again.

I'm doing well in every area except one: I can't seem to trust any of the men I go out with. My ex-husband put me through so much pain and suffering that now I shy away from them. When I start seeing somebody nice, either he does something to scare me off, or I *think* he did something wrong or that he's *going* to do something wrong. It could be something very small, something another person wouldn't even notice, and to me it says, "He's going to hurt you." And I run away or just turn off and become cold toward him so he runs away. I don't want to go through life alone, but right now I feel like damaged goods. I guess until I stop feeling that way, I'm not going to be able to keep a relationship going.

Rebecca

How can you take that chance? How can you allow another man to reject you, put you through the nightmare you've just managed to come through?

You feel that you're never going to go through that hell

again—not only don't you want to *date*, you don't even want to sit next to a man on the bus. Yes, I understand, but I think you have to fight the impulse to bury yourself at home. To my mind, you're the loser.

I think it's far better to be a fighter and make something of your life. I'm not saying it's easy, but if you don't do it, nobody will do it for you.

And yet, I'm very aware that there are women who live happily without men or romance in their lives. If this is your choice, if it's truly what you want and not what you're settling for, I have no negative thoughts about it. It's just not my way.

My friend Bernadette, who lives in London, married very young and divorced. Bernadette says, "I don't want to have to worry about somebody else. I want to take care of myself, eat what I like to eat, when I like to eat it."

No one can argue; she has a wonderful life. She entertains, she travels, she has tons of friends. She loves the theater and travels in theatrical circles. And she's completely free. She doesn't have to cater to anyone else, and she certainly doesn't have to take the kind of abuse men too often dish out to their wives.

The truth is, I think that either extreme is no good: being without a man all your life, or being unable to survive without one for more than a short time. Abigail* stayed much too long, if you ask me, in a marriage with an abusive man. She told me that every time she went to dinner with her husband she'd be shaking with fear. The deal with him was, if he didn't have a good time at the party—if he was bored and not well entertained—he came home and let *her* have it. He'd beat her up. It was obviously her fault, and he expressed his opinion with his fists. The poor woman used to call ahead to check the seating arrangements and beg the hostess to seat her husband next to so-and-so, whom he liked, because if he had a dull evening she paid for it.

She wound up becoming an alcoholic; eventually, she went to a clinic and got control of her drinking problem.

It seemed, however, that she wasn't able to get control of her marriage and the miserable coward she was married to. She came to me very depressed one day, and even though she'd never worked at a job in her life, I offered to hire her at the Plaza Hotel. "It might not be the best job you could have," I told her, "but it will bring you fifty or sixty thousand a year. If you leave the marriage, your husband *has* to give you something. The kids are fourteen and sixteen, you've stuck it out long enough." I was trying to prove to her she *could* make it without the creep.

She was too afraid.

The family moved away. She'd visit every half year or so, then we'd lose touch.

Out of the blue, one day I got an invitation to her wedding. I didn't even know she had gotten a *divorce*.

It turned out she'd been single only about six months. Barely half a year after her divorce she was getting married again. She told me she'd known the man during her marriage, just as a friend, and had gotten to know him more intimately after her divorce, but still, I worry. I hope she's not jumping into another marriage too quickly. Abigail is the kind of woman who has to be married to feel secure. She knows her husband will provide for her, she'll have bread on her table, clothes in her closet. That's why she couldn't leave her husband until she had another situation lined up.

Hopefully she's happy. Whether she really loves this new man or just married him for security remains to be seen. I wish her all the luck, but I would be a little more careful. I wish Emily had been too:

My first husband and I eloped when we were eighteen. Everyone said we wouldn't last a year. We lasted twenty-

208

five years, until I buried him. His passing left me very well off, but very lonely. I had quite a few suitors come knocking at my door, and I married one of them—out of loneliness, not love, I realize now. Shortly after the wedding I found out he'd been in and out of drug programs all his life. Many people knew this, but nobody told me. Apparently he was clean when I married him, but he didn't *stay* clean. You can't imagine the hell he put me through. Lucky for me I had a good lawyer looking out for my interests, so when we got a divorce, my ex-husband didn't take me to the cleaners.

Emily

Although by far the greatest number of letters I get are from women, I do get some poignant letters from men. They have the same feelings of mistrust, of anger. They suffer, too, when the marriage breaks up, just like we do.

My ex-wife of ten years and mother of three wonderful children left me for another man two years ago. My children were three, six, and nine. It took many friends and people with hearts to put my pieces back in place. Finally I am ready to explore new relationships again, to fill the void in a very loving and caring heart.

Peter

By the way, don't listen to the people who quote those awful statistics about there being only three men for every six hundred women, and half of those men are in jail. If remarriage is what you want, I firmly believe you can have it.

March 2nd I will celebrate twenty-two years in a wonderful second marriage—something I could never have imagined thirty years ago, when I was hurting so bad.

Nancy

The only way to go into a marriage is with the absolute certainty that it is forever. Otherwise there's no point. You have to believe that this is what you want for the rest of your life.

And then you pray.

Some women write me that they'll never get married again, and some say they cannot be without a man. I understand both points of view, but I fall somewhere in between. For myself, I don't feel I have to be married; I don't need a man to support me financially or to help with my career. I certainly don't need a man to have children with—I have three beautiful children—but I like having romance in my life. I need the friendship and the companionship. I like the sharing that goes with family life. I like having someone loving at my side.

As far as marriage goes, I never say never. But right now, I can get the best of marriage—sex, sharing, fun, affection—without all the Sturm und Drang. Like my girlfriend Antoinette.* Antoinette is dating a wonderful man, but I don't think she'll marry him. "Why should I?" she says when we talk about it. "I have a 'friend' to sleep with, to be with, to have fun with. What's the point of getting married? For what?"

And when she says she never wants to go through that distribution of property again, I see her point. God forbid you marry a man and he winds up suing you for your own money! We all ask ourselves if we really want to risk going through the horror of divorce again. And once you are on your own for a long time, you become used to pleasing yourself.

That's partly why I don't believe it's healthy for a woman to be alone for too long. There are women who prefer it that way, and God bless them. They're happy— I'm happy for them. But on the whole, I think we were made to be together, two halves that fit, yes? But the longer you are alone . . . I won't say the more selfish you get, but it does get harder to live with someone else. I'm not in that stage, but I have friends who are. To them it's a big "Who needs it?"

I do.

But at the same time, don't think I'm not wary. I am.

My first romance after being divorced didn't last very long. When we met, he was married. I wouldn't get involved with him. I don't date married men. I don't need it and don't want it. We're not talking about the odd lunch, dinner, or drink but about the kind of dating that is the beginning stage of a romantic relationship.

This man would call and say, "Ivana, can I take you for a drink or dancing?"—a perfect gentleman. But I turned him down. Not only wouldn't I "date" him until he separated from his wife, I made it very clear that I didn't want people to think he left his wife for me. If he wanted to leave her, fine, but it had to be for reasons of his own, because his marriage wasn't working; I'm not a home wrecker. And then after a few months went by, he could join me, but as a free man.

He left her. But for a while there he was going back and forth between us, partly because he had a guilty conscience, but mostly because she was deeply involved in his business and he was afraid that with her knowledge she would take him to the cleaners.

I wouldn't stand for it. He couldn't come from his wife to me and vice versa. A lot of men like it that way—a wife and mistress. It's perfect. For them, not for me. I called it quits. He went back to his wife. He was lucky she took him back. I wouldn't have!

I don't think that relationship would have lasted anyway, because this gentleman was very disturbed by the press coverage that I live with, which is a normal part of my life by now. I understand that—it can be a regular zoo and very hard to take. I show up someplace and the next day it's all over the papers, Ivana and her handsome new beau—story *and* pictures! And they are all over him, trying to find out how much he's worth, what brand of soap he uses. His privacy is totally invaded.

In order to have any kind of relationship with me the man has to be very secure in himself, preferably someone who has achieved on his own. If he starts to compete with me, if he's at all insecure about the publicity, about money, then it just won't work for us. If he's a man of achievement and he's confident about his own worth, then it won't bother him that I'm on the front page of the newspaper and people ask for my autograph. He won't be threatened or intimidated by another person's fame. Hopefully he would be my biggest cheerleader (and I would be his).

I have a friend who is a superstar. The press covers her every move. But she's managed to have a love affair that's been going on for five years now and not a soul knows about it. He's something big in the banking world. Bankers are notoriously understated people who keep the lowest profile they can. Publicity would mean an end to their relationship and she knows it. She's photographed constantly, and yet he's never caught in the picture with her!

"How do you do that?" I asked her with admiration.

She let me in on a few of her little "techniques" and I thought they were ingenious. She and her lover manage a lovely social life—they attend the opera, balls, dinners—but they never *arrive* anywhere together. After the opera or the play or the ballet starts, he slips into a seat next to her. The photographers can't take pictures inside the theater, and anyway, there's only so much they can make out of two people who arrive and leave separately but happen to be sitting next to each other. When they leave, they go in separate cars so there's no photo of them together.

In the media, no photo equals no romance.

I thought that was neat, and when the situation calls for it, I do the same thing. If I'm seeing someone I don't want the press to know about or someone who's publicity-shy, I come a few minutes early and let them take all the photos they want of the dress and necklace and hairdo— whatever they want. Then I go to my seat. And when somebody sits at my side there's no way of knowing whether it's because we arranged it that way or it just happened. There's really no way to tell, is there?

And then there's that small percentage of men who would *die* to go out with me precisely because I have media attention. They want all that attention, they crave their fifteen minutes of fame, and they can't wait for the photographers to mob us. You know what they say, it takes all kinds. . . .

I have to laugh, though, because with all the attention the press lavish on me, all the time and money they spend figuring out what I'm up to, they so often get it wrong. More than once they've had me carrying on a passionate love affair with the wrong man. I never have an affair with more than one man at a time.

One time I was in the Swissair first-class lounge waiting for a flight to Zurich. I got to the airport in New York quite early, so I sat down to make calls. I telephoned the kids for one more good-bye-I-love-you; my assistant to go over some last-minute things. While I was on the phone, this gorgeous man walks into the lounge: tall, rugged face with a little scar on the side of his cheek—totally fabulous, an Omar Sharif type. You knew he was from somewhere exotic. He took a seat. But I could feel him staring at me. I paid no attention.

There was a Geneva flight just before mine, and when they called it, he got up and left. I thought, that's the end of that. A few minutes later they called my flight. I had asked for a seat in the first row, 1A or B or C or D, because in the wide-body no one has to pass in front of you and you have a lot of space for your legs. I was exhausted and I planned to go to sleep as soon as we sat down so I could get in seven hours of shut-eye before we landed. I had requested no drinks, no food—just a blanket, a pillow, and quiet. When I got on, though, I saw that Swissair had substituted a smaller plane, and in this aircraft, the seats I had asked for were the *worst!* There was just a tiny little space for my long legs. I called the stewardess over and told her politely, "This is unacceptable, can you do something?"

She said she'd try, after everybody settled down.

After take-off they came to me and said, "Madame, we have a seat where you'll be more comfortable."

They moved all my stuff and I headed for the new seat. Oh no! Who's my seatmate? The man from the lounge. The Starer.

I thought, That's it, I'm trapped. Now he's got me captive. He's going to tell me all about himself, he's going to make the moves on me, and all I wanted was sleep.

And sure enough, I sit down and he introduces himself. I nod.

"I know you," he says. (You'd have to be in the outback for the last five years not to recognize me.) "As a matter of fact, we are lovers."

"No, we're not." (*That* I was sure of. I'd know.)

"According to the columnists we are. My name is Manoucher Khanlari."

And I started to laugh. I recognized his name from those very gossip columns he was talking about. But despite the "rumors" and stories of our "hot affair," I'd never met him until this very moment. He told me that when the story broke, a New York reporter called him in Geneva: "I understand you're having an affair with Ivana. Can you comment?"

He answered, "I've never met Ivana in my life and I'm certainly not having an affair with her."

So what did they print? That Manoucher didn't want to comment because gentlemen don't kiss and tell. They just don't take no for an answer. Can you imagine if we'd been spotted together on that plane? Would any journalist in the world have believed that we were seated together *purely by accident!*

Sometime later Manoucher—who turned out to be perfectly charming—came to New York on a business trip and called me. I had a table that night for the opening of the ballet and one woman had called to say her husband was ill and she was coming alone. I had an empty place at my table, so I asked Manoucher if he would like to go. He said he would be delighted and offered to pick me up.

We had a drink; we went to the ballet. The next day the press went crazy: Ivana and her new beau.

And our famous reporter who broke the original story got to say: "As I wrote in my column a long time ago, remember? Ivana has a hot new romance. . . ."

Manoucher called me the next day and told me he'd had fifty phone calls from reporters asking all kinds of personal questions. He is quite a private person and he hated it.

I said, "Welcome to the world of Ivana."

Even if I called a press conference and swore on the lives of my children that we weren't having an affair, they wouldn't believe me. The poor man ran like hell. He just couldn't take it. Believe me, I understand. But it's part of my life and the man has to be able to live with it.

Before I begin to *think* of being involved physically and emotionally, I want to know everything about the person. Riccardo and I went out for probably three months before we even kissed—and I'd known him for a while when we started dating. What can I tell you, I'm very careful. When we first met, I was dating somebody else. Riccardo had just gotten a divorce from his wife after having been separated for five years. That's how it works in Italy. I thought of him as a friend in the beginning, but later on we got romantic.

Riccardo says that on our first few dates, he felt like he was being interviewed—and he was! I really grilled him. I wanted to find out where he stands, what he likes, who he is. He tells me now he felt like a schoolboy, but let's face it, you're not out with a man because you need someone to buy you dinner. This is someone you might be romantically interested in and you're out with him in order to get to know him. Before I got serious with Riccardo, I had a pretty good idea what he was about. Look, you do research before almost any important project. What could be more important than this? As I said, there are no guarantees, but this way hopefully you can avoid unpleasant surprises. The good surprises I wish you every day.

Many of my friends seem to marry the same man over and over. Not literally the same—they're different people, but they look the same, have the same habits, and you can hardly tell husband number three from numbers one, two, and four. Tycoons in particular seem addictive. After a woman divorces one, she'll frequently marry another.

On one level I understand it. Tycoons are fabulous; they're wealthy, smart, brilliant. But nothing is free. Any person who's a genius of some kind is usually messed up in some other way. That's what I've found, anyway.

I personally don't want a tycoon. I had enough with the one I had to last me a lifetime.

I'm kidding. I'll take life as it comes, and I make it an ironclad rule not to rule things out up front. But I am aware that I'm not looking for the same qualities as before.

What do I like in a man? Well, great energy for one thing. He has to be smart—I'm not saying he has to be a genius, but I can't be with a man when my face falls into the pasta plate because I can't stay awake. He has to amuse me somehow. Look for somebody you can have fun with, laugh with, and have a good conversation with. That's just about the most important thing—except, of course, that the man respect you and treat you with the utmost courtesy. And as I've said, in my case, he has to be very secure in himself to live in the world I live in.

I don't care particularly whether he has money. I'm not looking to support a man, but whether he has five million dollars or ten or twenty, who cares? Past a certain point, if he has twenty or a hundred million it doesn't make a difference. How many steaks can you eat, cars can you buy, homes can you own? He has to be able to support his home and his children. Certainly I don't need a boyfriend to support my children. I'm lucky that in my case how much money he has isn't a factor.

I do look for achievement in a man. I like "doers." They're exciting to be around. When you're with them, everything is punched up, quicker and livelier and bubblier, because they're so smart. And because they're smart, they've made a lot of money. Once you have money, you usually want and get power, so they've got brains, money, and power—an unbeatable combination in my book.

So what if they don't look like lifeguards. These men can show you a good time in a way that a surfer never could, no matter how golden his tan or luscious his lips. There are certain pastimes you can indulge in only if you have money. I suppose polo is one, although I have no interest in it. I prefer collecting art. Anybody can go to auctions in Sotheby's and Christie's, but to collect you need serious money. Many people who achieve wealth wind up being collectors, whether of paintings, sculpture and other fine art, antique furniture, antique rugs, or other objets d'art. In your twenties and thirties you can be interested and observe, but in order to actually participate you have to wait till later when the fruits of your labors bring you enough money to buy. I think mature men are more interesting and have more wherewithal to give you an interesting life.

Looks in a man really don't matter to me. What I can't stand is men who say, "My nose is too big, isn't it?" Come on, haven't you worked that out by now? I love the guy with the big nose who brags about it. "Isn't my nose fabulous?" He's secure. He likes himself.

Likewise, the man's religion doesn't mean much to me. Everyone has to have somebody to pray to in order to get through life, but exactly what it is doesn't matter to me. I'm Catholic and I believe in God. I'm certainly thankful for all the blessings I've been given. When I have trouble, I pray. I get letters all the time from very religious people telling me to leave everything in God's hands. That's true only up to a point. Don't think you can sit in your living room and God will deliver your paycheck. He'll guide you, but he won't pay your rent.

As to whether there is life after death—I believe there is, but I'm in no rush to see what it's like. Some widows write me that they are looking forward to joining their deceased spouse. I think that's great, but what's the hurry? If there is another life after this I'm sure it's good, too. But let's live this one fully and enjoy it as best we can. Then when the time comes, you can enjoy the next one too. As I always say, there's nothing wrong with old money, and nothing wrong with new money either.

My ex-husband is Protestant and I never had a problem with it. If my man were Jewish it would make no difference to me. With an Arab man, I'd have a little problem since I have no intention of being one of four wives. I suppose there's nothing wrong with it if that's the custom of your country, but it's not mine.

Everybody after the age of thirty-five has some sort of "baggage," don't they. Kids, for one—and as adorable as they may be, if you've got two and he's got three and they hate each other's guts, it's tough.

You have an ex-spouse—maybe even more than one.

You have in-laws—the grandparents don't leave the picture because of the divorce.

On the other hand you're a lot smarter than you were.

More secure, too. I'm generally more secure in myself now than I was when I was younger, and so are most of my friends. We have a better understanding about how the world works, how we ourselves work, and how we fit into the larger world around us. I believe that when you're ready to allow a man into your life, whether for marriage or romance, you'll be able to make much better choices this time around.

Whatever the reasons you married the first time, you probably didn't take a close look at what interests each of you had. The second time you approach things a little more intelligently. You want somebody who can keep up with you, who is interested in what interests you. I would not go out with a man if I knew he lived for golf. Maybe he pretends otherwise during our courtship, and maybe it lasts through the first few months of our marriage. But sooner or later, I guarantee you he's on the golf course for the rest of his life. And then what will I do?

In the same way, I wouldn't keep company with a man who hates to travel. I love to travel and I'm looking for someone with the same interest. That's how you get companionship. When you're young, you marry for love. You don't really take a good look at the person. You follow your heart and suddenly you have kids of your own and it's ten years later and you realize you don't have that much in common with this person. That makes a marriage very hard to sustain. I happen to think it's the most common cause of trouble in a marriage, not having any interests in common. In the old days, in my parents' generation, people stayed together no matter what. But today there are so many temptations.

As I've said, if you really want to be married again, and you put your mind to it and make an effort, you'll be able to. It's not that difficult. Hopefully, you'll have learned from the bad experience you had how to conduct yourself next time and choose someone more compatible with you.

Whether you remarry or just have a romance, sooner or later you're going to want to go to bed with him. And at first that's likely to be a very scary prospect.

When you first start going out after your divorce, all you want from the man is that he *not* lay a finger on you. You live in fear that he might make a move on you, because you're just not ready.

I have to say a word here about the man who thinks that if he takes you for dinner or a movie, you have to go to bed with him, since he paid your way. Well, honey, you can afford your own dinner and your own movie. If you run across somebody like that, don't fall for it. You don't need that headache. After what you've been through you don't want to go to bed with a man unless he really wants to be with *you*, he likes you for yourself, not just as a bed partner, and you of course should be crazy about him too. You want to make love with him, but you also want him to be someone you can talk to and discuss things with. So just avoid men who make you feel pressured. You had enough pressure with your separation and divorce, don't you think?

This is one matter in which you have every right to please yourself and only yourself. *You* decide who to go to bed with, based only on what you feel like doing. If you feel like doing nothing, that's exactly what you do. You don't owe that man a thing. He took you out for a nice dinner and hopefully you were fantastic company. Even if he's taken you out three, four, *ten* times, you still don't have to have sex with him. If your company weren't sufficient, he wouldn't be taking you out. If you're getting the feeling that you have to supply sex in exchange for his hospitality, that's a tip-off that you're being pressured, even if it's very subtle.

Don't let yourself be controlled again. Maybe you went to bed with your husband out of duty when you were a married woman, but you're not married anymore. Now there should be no such thing as dutiful sex in your life. You have sex when and where you want to.

If there comes a time when it seems like a nice idea, you're in the mood, and the man appeals to you in that way . . . fine. Otherwise, no.

I never went out with men who expected more than I wanted to give. Until I felt it was right, I didn't do a thing. Any amount of time I wanted to take was fine. Only when I felt completely comfortable might something happen between us. Sometimes it never did; I just didn't feel like going to bed with that person. I'm not a teenager at the mercy of my hormones. I enjoy sex, but I want to know what and when and with whom.

Sometimes women are afraid that if they don't "give" the man sex he'll drop them. I say, so what? You shouldn't be with a creep like that in the first place. If he's just going out with you because he wants to get you in the sack, forget it.

But there will come a time, I hope, when you have met a lovely new man and you're ready and eager to make love with him.

The first time you make love with a man after your divorce is a difficult and tricky experience. Don't be devastated if it doesn't go well. This probably won't be the greatest sex of your life. Usually the woman is so scared she can't relax. You see, the only man you really know in that way is your ex-husband. With him you had a familiar routine.

Now you're with somebody new, and a new man might have all kinds of tricks that you never heard of. Many women are afraid they won't be "good enough"; that they'll be lacking in some way: What if I don't know what the other girls know these days? Maybe if I knew what the other girls know, my husband wouldn't have left me.

My feeling about those fears is that if you *expect* to have them you won't be so thrown by them. They're natural, and they pass. So the first couple of times you didn't feel the earth move—so what? Give yourself a little more time to feel completely at ease with the man, and I'm sure things will improve. After all, it's the "newness" of the relationship that's exciting.

I love that feeling of getting ready for a date with a man you don't know very well but you like, and you feel he likes you. That delicious possibility that you might become intimate makes you hum to yourself as you get yourself gorgeous for him.

This isn't like the bad old days when you could predict—with your eyes blindfolded, your hands tied behind your back, and plugs in your ears—every move, sexually speaking, that your husband would make.

But with *him*, this new man . . . you can't predict what's going to happen at all. That's what makes it so delicious and exciting.

However, trying new things does leave you open to experiencing something you may not like. Should it happen that you find yourself in bed with a man who wants to do something you're not interested in, just say, "That's not something I want to do." And that's perfectly fine. Some people enjoy being creative sexually and that's fine too. But if it's uncomfortable or, God forbids, hurts—just say so. Both of you should stop and talk about it. Usually the other person wants the sex to be nice for you too, so he won't force you to do something you don't enjoy.

And isn't it nice to have somebody again!

You rediscover all the small pleasures—flirting on the telephone, sending and getting little notes and faxes. One lovely trick is to sneak little notes into secret places so he'll find them. Just make sure it's a place *only* he will find it, especially if it's going to make him blush.

If you've been alone for any length of time, you might have to relearn some of your skills. As we all know, men have big egos—*huge* egos, actually. Naturally, you're not trying to encourage this, but it's fun to sort of *massage* their egos a little bit. When you're married, you figure, My husband knows I'm crazy about him, I don't have to say it. But in a romance, you can give those little compliments I think are so important.

Say to him, "You look so handsome today."

"I love you in that color, it makes your eyes so blue" (or brown or green).

"What is it that makes you smell so nice?"

That's a way of saying you notice and you care.

When you've been dating someone for a while and you're comfortable together, it's nice to take a romantic trip. If you ski, rent a ski condo or a chalet. You can curl up in front of the fire with a nice bottle of wine and just be really romantic with each other. Mmm. Lovely. Sometimes it's nice to go south and just spend time together, skinny-dipping, walking on the beach.

If things are really getting serious between you, don't forget to do the list-of-interests trick. Sit down with paper and pencil and make a list of things you like to do and how he feels about them, and things he likes to do that you *hate*, just as you did with your ex. You'll see very quickly how compatible you are with him. Somehow if you see it on paper, it becomes clear to you. If you are aware from the beginning that he lives for bowling and you're an outdoor person, you should know going in that no matter what he says, he won't give it up for you. He might go for walks in the park with you for half a year or so if you really make a federal case out of it, but it won't last.

Again, always watch out for drugs and for alcohol abuse. I believe you can't be too cautious in these areas.

Also, make sure he has a way of making money. He doesn't have to be a billionaire, but he should at least be self-supporting, so, God forbid, if you do marry him and the marriage ends, he won't sue you for your money.

And never date a married man. If you've been on the other side of that one, you know how much pain you're causing his wife, and his children if he has them. It's just not right. You don't have to go looking for problems; you've had enough in your life, haven't you? Find a man who's free. Of course, if he's divorced or widowed and he has children, that's okay. Hopefully you like them and they will like you—or learn to. Children are a part of life and I would never hold them against anybody. I believe that unless they really are unholy brats, you'll eventually win them over with kindness, sympathy, and a large dose of fun.

Beware of a nasty little trap in your divorce settlement called a "cohabitation" clause, which says that you get alimony only as long as you're not living with another man. This clause has brought more grief to more women! It's a handy-dandy way for a man to keep a rein on his ex-wife, an excuse to dig into her private life, and an additional string tying her to him—just one more reason to get a lump settlement, and then you never have to worry what he knows, what he thinks, what his opinion is.

I like to talk to my kids about my plans and my doings. They're interested. And also, I don't want them to find out what their mother is up to from the newspapers. But I did have a talk with them and explained that my private life is my business, and I would please ask them not to discuss what I do and where I go. "Talk about yourselves, your schools, what you've done, your friends. But don't talk about me and what I'm trying to do with my life."

I told my kids, "Your daddy is the only father you will ever have. See him, be with him as much as you want. But what each of us does is private. If he should ask you anything about me, you can say: 'Mommy never asks us about your doings. If you want to know what she's up to, why don't you call her and ask her?' "

But, no matter how well you've prepared your children, don't be surprised if they blurt out something to your ex about your new love interest. Not out of animosity— they're not really trying to "tell" on you—but if they've seen you go out on a date or met the man, that's big news in their lives and they'll be sure to pass it on.

That's why I say, if you're just starting to date someone, don't let the kids know about it. I don't believe your children should meet a casual date; there's no need for it. Why not meet him someplace else instead of your home? That way you won't have to introduce them. In fact, I wouldn't let them have much to do with each other until you're absolutely sure of your feelings and his.

Many of the men I saw socially after my divorce my kids had known from before. They were in our home while I was married and now they're escorts for the evening. It feels very natural to everybody. But I know that many people bring the man into the kids' lives when they've had several dates and plan to continue seeing each other, at least for a while. I can't really quarrel with that, but I still wouldn't let him get deeply involved in the children's lives so soon. (On the other hand, if you're really serious about a man, that's something else. You *want* him to spend time with your kids so you can see how he interacts with them and if the kids like him.)

Children will absorb their mother's antagonism toward

their father no matter how hard she tries to keep it from them. There may well be a period of time when they don't feel warm toward the man who's making Mommy cry all the time. If their relationship with their father isn't good, the children may be hungry for a man.

But that's no reason to let them get attached to somebody *you're* not permanently attached to. I feel the children have had enough instability in their lives and you shouldn't subject them to "Uncle Bob" if he's going to be followed by "Uncle Steve" and "Uncle Matt." Since you're not at your most stable—and who would be after going through what you have—he probably won't be around them enough for them to get terribly attached to him, but even so, they'll wonder what happened to that nice man who brought all those presents.

And if they *do* like him, and *do* get attached to him, you'll have the added burden of knowing that if you break up with him, it might be very hard on your kids. It'll be even worse when he goes out of their lives. They'll have to suffer through another rejection. And this one they will blame you for . . . no matter how unconsciously.

So I say: Enjoy, but leave the kids out of it until you really think this man is going to be with you for life, or at least for the next ten years. I hope you'll be having the most wonderful romance with your new man—you're crazy about him, he's crazy about you—but I think you always have to be very discreet where the children are concerned. They know you're divorced, but I can almost guarantee you that on some subconscious level in their minds they still see you as married to their father. What's more, they may continue to see you that way for years to come. What you do with your new sweetie is private. I think you have to be extra careful—even more so than if he were just a casual friend. I don't believe you should ever allow your children to see a man so much as sitting

226

on your bed, let alone making himself at home in your bedroom.

True, I did say that you deserve a sex life.

I meant it.

But I never said it would be easy, did I?

Still, there's always a way. All you have to do is think. Maybe you can arrange for a sitter and stay over at his place. Perhaps you have to forgo "all-nighters" for a while unless you can manage to send the kids away to relatives or friends for the weekend. But there's nothing wrong with "love in the afternoon," if that's when you can arrange a private meeting.

A little ingenuity goes a long way—and a few obstacles never hurt a love affair. On the contrary, they add spice. Remember sex with your husband? You knew what he was going to do before he did it. He knew what you were going to do before you did it. You both knew when and where; it was hardly worth the effort. Now, when you have to make all these arrangements and keep these secrets . . . what fun it is when you finally get together!

Eventually, there may come a time when you want to bring the children and your boyfriend together. A little planning will make it go much more smoothly. You want to make it appear as spontaneous and natural as possible. That means he shouldn't arrive bearing armloads of gifts—or any presents at all, really. Some people start in giving gifts right away, but I don't believe in that. Let him see them a few times first and get to know them a little bit. Then he'll know what interests they have and he can bring a small present, a T-shirt or baseball cap, a CD of the music the child likes. This kind of gesture can mean quite a bit to children. It tells them that the person has taken the trouble to figure out what will please them, and you know how good that makes *you* feel, don't you? It will give your kids that same warm feeling—even if they are reluctant to admit it. Also, children are like homing pigeons when it comes to presents. They just adore getting things, and the size of the gift has very little effect on how much pleasure they get out of it. We've all seen little ones play with the wrapping and not the toy.

I stress that your new sweetie should *not* be giving your kids expensive toys at this stage. He's not trying to buy them; he's trying to *win* them. The first you do through money, the second you do through attention. If the man is patient and sensitive he can slowly win the children over without pushing himself on them—which is the surest way to alienate them.

There are cases, however, where the kids just won't warm up to him. You're all but hanging yourself from the ceiling, you're tying yourself in knots, and nothing works. They just don't like him. What can you do about that?

Not much. Just let them be.

If despite all your efforts, the kids won't warm up to your new honey, it's unfortunate, but you can't force them. However, you'll all be better off if you can get them at least to make friends. One woman I know is dying to go on vacation with her man *and* her kids, but she has to choose between them or she'll have the vacation from hell. It's important for your own comfort that the man get along with your children, and you should do all you can to make this happen. But you can't really expect your kids to fall into the arms of this new man. Why should they? Unless you've brought home Sylvester Stallone or Bart Simpson or some other kids' hero, they're more than likely to resist the whole idea of a rival for your time and affection.

One thing you can do is have a heart-to-heart talk with them. (Like all "heart-to-hearts" with kids, this works best if you're in the habit of discussing things with them and the channels of communication are routinely kept open. I firmly believe that you should start chatting as early as possible and keep doing it. That way when either side has a problem, it's natural to bring it up.)

Tell your kids that whatever-his-name-is is a very nice man, although it's clear from the way they're acting that they don't think so. Ask them to give him a chance. Appeal to their better nature. Wasn't there a time when they wanted to be friends with someone and the other person wasn't that interested? Didn't they wish that person would take the time to get to know them?

But of course, that's not the heart of the problem. The heart of the problem is, their mommy is going out on dates. And I think you have to address it. "Maybe it feels funny to have Mommy going out with a man, but I am divorced and it's okay for me to do it. It's perfectly fine, and you know what? It makes me happy. You know how you enjoy birthday parties or tennis matches (or whatever)? Grownups like to go out for the evening. That's our pleasure."

No matter what you do, there's a chance they'll hate his guts anyway. But work on it. I was lucky: I had no problems in this area. My friends played with my kids and were very nice to them, and my kids are exceptionally friendly, sociable people. They're used to having lots of people around; they were raised that way. Every weekend in Mar-a-Lago I'd give sit-down dinners for thirty-five, as well as having people over for lunch, for tea, for screenings of movies—not to mention having my girlfriends in for exercise classes.

In Trump Tower I also entertained a lot: big parties, small parties, cocktail parties, luncheons, charity events. I always insisted the children be around. Often when I had a sit-down dinner the children, who had eaten before, of course, would come in and say, "Can I have a chair on the side and stay for the dinner and chat?" My kids have

always been surrounded by people, and they speak to this
one and discuss with that one.

From the age of two or three, they were never shy;
there was no peeking out from behind Mommy's skirt.
Ivanka is a very polished child. She knows how to greet
people, how to make the small talk. (I have to tell you
I've been calling that "the small chat," which makes people smile. I don't know quite why—small talk, small
chat—seems about the same to me. But I've been cor-
rected.) You can have a wonderful conversation with her
or with Eric or with Donny. They introduce themselves,
start to talk, mingle with people—automatically, without
thinking about it. It's their habit. And it stood them in
good stead when I divorced. But not all children are that
flexible, and I can understand a child resenting that her
mother has separated and suddenly there's a new papa,
or a man who wants to be the new papa, even though
my kids didn't give me a hard time. Many women write
to me about problems in this area, and there's not much
I can suggest except to speak to the child.

Ask him or her, "Is it that you don't like *this* man, or
that you wouldn't like *any* man I was with? I have to
know, because I want to have a man in my life. I'm a
woman and that's how we are made. Women want to be
with men, men want to be with women. Without that I
wouldn't have you children. I can't go on without a man
the rest of my life. You have to give me a chance, because
I want to be happy too and this man makes me happy.
So please do try. . . . I'm doing everything I can for you.
Try to do this for me."

Maybe they won't jump for joy around him, but they
won't be nasty. And you may have to be content with
that. Some people would thank God for that much. Oh,
the things kids do to Mama's boyfriend or Papa's girlfriend! They can be so horrible!

I've heard of kids putting honey on his or her chair.

230

The bucket of water over the door is always good.

Girls, who can twist their daddies around their fingers, are fond of suddenly bursting into floods of tears when left alone for a minute with The Girlfriend. Daddy comes running in a panic! "What did you do to my daughter?" "I didn't touch her, I swear!"

How many girlfriends have been pushed into swimming pools? Just after they've had their hair done seems to be the time of choice.

Sometimes the kids don't do anything—and I mean *nothing!* They ignore the new person completely. Oh, they'll pass the salt, but that's all.

I heard about a man who promised he'd take his kids out to dinner *alone,* and then he brought Her along. The kids spent the entire dinner pointing out beautiful and desirable women in the restaurant whom their father could date. Apparently the fact that he was *already* dating someone escaped them . . . or they acted as if it had.

If my kids were acting this way, I'd say, "Come on, kids, be dignified." My kids have been raised knowing how important dignity is to me, so it has an effect.

There may come a time when you or your spouse will remarry and even have other children. In that case, the one who is remarrying must give every thought and care to the children you already have. The parent who will have the new baby must speak to his/her children and explain that even though he or she is going to have another child, nothing will change the love he or she has for them or their security and position.

I've said many times that for my part, my family is complete. I don't think I will have another child. But Donald had a child after our divorce and has since married the child's mother, and I'm often asked how my children reacted to this turn of events. I find that my children's lives have not been very much affected because I

231

explained to them, and so did their father, that their lives will not change nor will his love for them. They are and will forever be his children. And you know, my children are not babies. They know that both their parents have gone on with their lives, and that's the way it should be.

When my husband's daughter was born, I raised the subject with Ivanka. (If it had been a boy, I would have been more likely to discuss it with my sons.) I asked her how she felt toward the new baby. Ivanka said, "This child didn't do anything wrong to anybody and I'm not going to be mean or nasty to her."

That was it. That was all the conversation we had about it. As far as the boys go, Donny never brought it up, but I can't imagine it has much weight in his sixteen-year-old life. Eric couldn't care less. He's a ten-year-old boy and he's interested in bicycles, tennis, and soccer, not cradles.

My children don't bring it up, and I don't either, because it's not my life. It's not my business. And if it doesn't worry the children, why should I bother about it?

If you are faced with this situation, you may have to help your child adjust to a new half-sibling—and maybe more than one. Perhaps you should follow Ivanka's lead, and impress upon your child that the baby didn't do anything wrong, and there should be no ill feelings, jealousy, or hatred toward the child. Of course, if your children are closer in age to the newcomer, this may be easier said than done. A lot depends on how their father handles it. Both of you have to assure and reassure the children— verbally, *in words,* actually *telling* them—that they are just as loved as before. Don't assume "they know" or "it goes without saying." It doesn't. Tell them. Again and again.

When their father remarried, my children spoke among themselves and agreed that while they would support their father all the time and in all ways, they did not want to celebrate this remarriage. And, therefore, they decided not to attend the wedding. However, I don't feel that Donald's relationship with our children has changed, nor do I expect it to change in the future. They go willingly to visit him and call him frequently.

While you were married, assuming neither of you was cheating, you probably weren't using anything, but if you go out in the world, you must use protection. I don't care if it's your fourteenth time with him or your twentieth or if the guy shows you signed references saying he's an angel. You must protect yourself. (The only exception is if he has had a recent negative AIDS test and you *know* he's sleeping only with you. But I say: Why take a chance? It's been known to happen that men lie. Are you willing to bet your life that he's telling the truth? I wouldn't.)

The first gift I got from my girlfriends after my separation was a pair of absolutely gorgeous earrings. They were presented to me at that Valentine's Day birthday luncheon I told you about earlier. The earrings were very unusual. I hadn't seen anything quite like them before, and said so. My friends practically laughed themselves under the table. I asked what was so funny. They couldn't speak!

Finally, somebody stopped laughing long enough to show me: The earrings were cunningly designed condoms. My friends were telling me to leave my broken marriage behind and get on with my life. But to keep it safe.

Nobody knows all there is to know about the AIDS virus and how it's transmitted. Until they know how to cure it, don't take any chances. I can't say this often enough: You must be aware, alert, and responsible. The man you're dating might be dating another five ladies. And who knows who was in his past? I hear that young women these days bring their own condoms on dates, and I'm all for it. Recently I read about a company that was making condoms in pretty little packets rather like herbal teas, for purchase by women. What a good idea!

233

You're probably embarrassed enough by the whole idea of having sex with someone other than your ex; the idea of asking him to use a condom seems impossible. To hell with the embarrassment. If you don't do it, you might die. I'm not working this hard to help you into a wonderful new life to see you pick up some awful disease that was completely avoidable.

If you get serious with the man, ask him to have an AIDS test, and of course you will do the same. By the way, if he's the one who brings it up, don't be mad, be grateful. You go for mammograms and Pap tests and stuff like that, don't you? An AIDS test should be part of your life in exactly the same way if you're sexually active. When you get a checkup, they're going to be taking blood anyway, so let them run one more test. Is there an easier way to protect your life?

I think a woman should make a point of getting herself tested immediately after her separation or divorce. If you know your man was fooling around, you go immediately, the minute you find out! Maybe he used protection, maybe he didn't. If he gave you a disease, you want to know about it right away. But even if you think he never looked at another woman, take the test. I did. It's only common sense in this day and age.

If you are a man who is dating or thinking of dating a woman who is newly divorced, please remember that she hasn't dated anyone for a long time. She has forgotten how it was done *then,* and for sure she doesn't know how it's being done now. She's feeling a little bit insecure.

Be charming; give her compliments—not phony ones, real ones; if they're phony, she'll know. If you can't find something to compliment her about then you shouldn't be going out with her in the first place.

Try to make her feel feminine; let her know you think she's sexy.

Be a gentleman at all times. That shows that you care, that you treat her with respect.

Above all, don't try to push her into having sex. She'll let you know when she's ready.

And if sex is not great, if it hasn't worked well between you, or she never does come around to sleeping with you, that's okay too. There are no guarantees in the bedroom— which leaves room for many nice surprises and some that are not so nice. We call that life.

Part 5

The Best Is Yet to Come

Chapter 12

My Recipe for Raising Kids

*M*y children are my jewels, my companions, and as they grow older, my best friends. People often ask me how my children managed to come through some difficult times in a very public manner and are turning out so well. I have some very strong opinions on child rearing, and I'm very proud of the job I did and am doing with my kids.

Being a mom is the only job I know of where you're on duty twenty-four hours a day, seven days a week, three hundred sixty-five days a year, with no time off for good behavior! People who don't have children often can't quite understand why we go through it. But those of us fortunate enough to be parents know: It's the most satisfying job in the world. And truly the most important. Nothing hurts quite as much as seeing your child in pain, whether physical or emotional. And nothing is quite as rewarding as seeing your child flourish and thrive.

I'm a great believer in keeping children busy. One reason I never get depressed is that I work so hard that at the end of the day I don't have the energy to breathe! I fill my day so full of appointments that at night when I ask myself what happened today, I have to think hard to remember everything. And I do the same thing with my kids. They simply can't get into trouble because their schedules are filled!

After school they have play dates, gymnastics, ballet lessons, computer lessons, piano lessons, French lessons— all kinds of different activities. They're constantly on the run, from school to karate, from karate to this or that. When they finally go to bed, they fall into a coma!

But they have no time to get into trouble.

Also, I feel better having them in supervised activities. In New York it's dangerous to hang around on the streets. Children have to be in some kind of planned and supervised activity, even if it's just ice-skating with a group of friends. I think it's wrong to just let them roam the streets. If you live in the suburbs or in a small town, that's something else, of course. And at the same time that they're doing all these lovely things they are trying them out to see what they might like. If you give the children millions of things to do, that's how they find out what they're good at. Eric loves woodworking and designing things. He might be very good at it. He'll find out by taking classes. My feeling is, even if your child never picks up a paintbrush again in his life, it's nice to take art lessons. They learn about the different paintings, great art, and artists; it adds something to their lives. If it turns out they can't draw, they haven't lost anything, and they've learned about a subject I think is very important. When they're out socially and people mention the Picasso exhibit or the Monet exhibit, they'll be able to take part in the conversation intelligently.

I encourage my children to try new things, but I don't necessarily go along with every whim or notion they take into their heads. As much as I tell them they can do any-

240

thing, *and* I believe in giving them the chance to try different things, I don't want them to engage in pastimes that have no future. The other day, Ivanka came to me and said she wanted to enroll one afternoon a week in field hockey. I said, "Ivanka, that's a boys' sport, you're not going anywhere with it. You get it in school anyway . . . that's enough. There's no future in it for you."

Eric wanted to do karate—fine. If Ivanka wanted to do karate, also fine. I have no problem with karate for girls. It's self-defense, and it's also great exercise. Field hockey she doesn't need. I think golf is a perfect sport, but fencing? I'd say, "Kid, don't waste your time."

However, if she *really* wanted to do it I'd let her. But if it's one of those little fads that disappears from one day to the next, I try to discourage it, or turn them toward a sport that would give them greater benefit. Ice skating, for example, is great exercise and it's social. You can do it with another child, your parents, whatever. You won't get many phone calls inviting you to play field hockey on a winter afternoon. But ice skating you can do in New York City—at the beautiful Wollman Rink in Central Park, which their father and I rebuilt during our marriage, or at my weekend home in Greenwich—almost anywhere.

Right now Ivanka is concentrating on making the swimming team at school and she plays the piano. She took ballet for a few years, but then she had grown too tall for ballet and she knew there would be no future in it for her, so she dropped it. I push the boys to try every sport there is. Eric goes to karate, ice skating, and hockey. All my kids play tennis and ski beautifully.

However, there are some things I consider a must and I give my children no choice about them. My kids have to learn to play an instrument, I don't care what it is. I prefer piano so that they can entertain people later on. But if Ivanka would want to study guitar instead, that's okay with me. Donny plays the drums. It's music, I suppose, but it seems kind of useless to me, unless he gets into a band. You really cannot entertain a house party on the drums. I like my children to be able to entertain when they're houseguests or have guests at their home. I think that's a wonderful social skill, but drums you can't shlep with you to a friend's country home. Eric plays the piano, which I think is more useful.

Languages are another must. As with music, my kids have no choice about *whether* they will study languages, but they can pick which ones—in addition to the ones I want them to have. If they want Japanese, it's okay with me, but they also have to learn to speak French. Ivanka will learn Italian and German when she goes to boarding school in Switzerland. Yesterday Donny called me from school and started speaking to me in Czech. He wanted to practice, so he wouldn't forget it. He loves that language and I'm sure that will be one place he'll travel to and eventually he might even have some business interests there. As is, the children spend one month a year in the Czech Republic. My mother spends a lot of time here and she speaks Czech with them, so it's almost a second home, a place with which they have warm family associations.

Lots of love, lots of fun, keep them very busy. That's pretty much my recipe for raising kids. And be a strong disciplinarian. I am. Much as I love them, my children know they can't get away with certain things. If you let them get away with small things, that's how they get out of control. My children have to do errands around the house. Ivanka goes and gets me the newspaper without question. And I say, "Thank you so much, Ivanka!" I lavish praise on her. She does things for me as much as I do things for her.

I find that some parents talk to their children as if they were servants. I get just as much cooperation—more, maybe—by asking them nicely. "Ivanka, would you do

me a favor and go with Tony [our driver] and buy tickets
for me?" She's obviously too young to go alone, but I've
given her a job to do, responsibility for something, and
she can be justly proud when she does it well.

I know parents who don't know what to do with their
kids. They don't seem to be able to manage them at all,
and finally, they simply send them away. Like a friend of
Donny's: His parents could not control him; he was totally
wild, out of line. They shipped him off to a military academy. He really shaped up there. Now it's "Yes, ma'am,
yes, sir." *And* he got a great education. So if parents truly
cannot deal with a child, I suggest they go find a really
strict school and let somebody else worry about it. At
least the child gets put on the proper track.

In my circles, I've seen parents send their kids shopping
with no instructions and no limits: Whatever you want,
buy it. I don't do that. I may be easygoing and generous
but I also have no trouble setting limits.

I'll give you an example. Donny called me from boarding school not long ago to ask if he could bring two of
his friends to Mar-a-Lago with us in March. They were
spending the first week of spring vacation in the Bahamas,
could they spend the second week with us? I teased him:
"Are they good kids?" Because he knows if they're not,
I call the parents and ship them out. But okay, he tells
me they're good kids and I say they can come.

A few minutes later Donny calls back: "Mom, can our
driver pick them up in Sarasota? They're landing there."

I said, "Absolutely not. If their parents want them to
come visit us, they have to arrange to get them to us.
Sure, I have people working for me, but I'm not going to
have them spend the day shlepping halfway across Florida to pick up two teenagers. I need them to do their
regular duties. You may bring guests, but you can't incon-
venience the rest of the family."

Donny was upset and started to argue with me.

243

I said firmly, "I'm going to worry about those boys *from the moment they arrive at our home*. Not before. Let the parents worry about how to get them there. They're two fifteen-year-old boys, can't they take a bus, for example? Do two kids need a chauffeured limousine to pick them up?"

He said they can't take a bus because they have to change buses. Okay, one kid alone I understand, maybe you don't want him to make a bus change. But two fifteen-year-old boys together, can't they figure out how to get from one bus to another? And if that doesn't sit well with the parents, let them arrange something else. While the children are with me they are my responsibility. But it starts and ends with their visit.

If I had to pick up all the kids who stay with us, I would go nuts. Ivanka and Eric have four or five kids sleep over in Greenwich just about every weekend. But the children make their own way to my house, and I take it from there. After the weekend, I bring them home with me and the parents can pick them up at their leisure. They know the kids are perfectly safe, they're comfortable and being looked after. I love having them around—as I've said, I like a houseful of kids, and I have very few discipline problems.

Sometime the kids get wild; all kids do. They're not really misbehaving, they're just very excited and they start to get a little silly. I go to them and say, "Girls, you can't do this in my house." If it's Eric, I say, "Boys, you cannot scream like that. You can't run through corridors or jump on furniture. But if you feel like jumping around, let's go outside. We'll ride bikes, play football or tennis—no problem. All you have to do is say the word."

And they obey. I don't have to talk to them very often. They're a little afraid of me. I like it that way. Maybe they're not afraid of their mothers, but I'm not their mother, and I will not put up with nonsense. They know I'm strong. Loving, but strong.

I think you have to be. Otherwise you'll wind up with spoiled-rotten kids, and there's nothing worse than a bratty kid, is there?

In general, I prefer that my kids bring their friends home to our houses rather than go to theirs. When they're with me I see what they eat, I know what they're up to, I know they're safe. When my children do go to someone else's house I get wonderful calls from the parents: "Ivana, your daughter is such a delight. She's fun, she's up for anything: 'You want to go there, that's great. There? That's great.' And she's so caring! And polite!" They can't praise her enough. She has fabulous manners. The boys too. They say thank you. They eat properly. They're friendly. All in all, they're joys to be with.

The boys and Ivanka are asked absolutely everywhere. Ivanka in particular is very popular. She's swamped with invitations and if she accepted them all I'd never see her! Since she is in school in New York City, I know her friends and their families well, so I feel very comfortable having her go to them for a weekend. But when Donny went to boarding school, he had a whole group of new friends whom I didn't know. I'd get a call: "Can I go this weekend to Max's?"

Who's Max? Who are his parents, where are they from? How will you get there? I don't want my kid driven by another kid just a couple of years older. That could be asking for trouble. As a parent, you worry.

In general I don't forbid the kids to go someplace unless I have a very good reason. I tell them, "Sure, you can go to Bermuda on a boat with your friend. But you're going to miss Mar-a-Lago." Since they love the month we spend there each year as much as I do, they usually don't want to be elsewhere. So I don't forbid and I don't say no. I

245

just give them reasons for what I think they should do. I might say, "Your grandmother's going to be there, I'm going to be there. I would love to be with you." Usually they decide to be with us and see their friends another time.

Last year Ivanka was invited by a friend to go skiing during spring break. I said, "Of course you can go. But then you won't be with *me*. I'll miss you."

On the other hand, I try to organize my life so when I'm going away, they are too. When I spent the weekend recently in Acapulco, Ivanka was with a school friend in Florida, Donny was at school on a "closed weekend," when the children cannot leave the school, and Eric was with his father. Then the following weekend, the children and I were all together in Greenwich.

Recently, Donny called to ask if he could stay in school for the weekend instead of coming to Greenwich with us. They were having a dance at school and he wanted to be there. A dance! He was giving me heart attacks! One minute it's those little robot toys; you blink your eyes and it's girls!

I had given Donny a telephone calling card when away at school because I wanted him to be able to call home as much as he wants; he can call his grandma in the Czech Republic, or anywhere else he wants to call: family, friends, I don't mind. I *want* him to keep in touch. However, in November, I got a bill that was triple what it should have been. And I saw that there were numerous calls to a town in Pennsylvania. Evening calls. Day calls. Morning calls.

I asked him, "Donny. Who are you calling there?" I thought maybe he was being taken advantage of by somebody using his telephone privileges.

He said, "I'm calling a friend."

I speak to everyone in a quiet tone. But now with my

son, I heard myself speaking even *more* softly. "Who's the friend?" I asked. I knew the answer.

"A girl," he said.

"A girlfriend?"

"Yes."

I asked her name, her parents' names. Then I said, "You have a girlfriend—that's fine. You're a young man, you're romancing a girl. Couldn't be more natural. I think it's great. But I have a problem. You want to play the big man, you want to romance your girl, you want to call her day and night? That's perfectly okay. But you have to pay for it.

"I give you forty dollars a week, deposited to your special account, which is very generous because the school advises twenty or twenty-five. That's to go and get a hamburger or pizza with the boys, when you don't want to eat in school.

"Now, whether you decide to go for pizza or buy the girl a present, or call her up on the phone—that's entirely up to you. But you have to manage it from that forty dollars a week.

"I'm going to pay this bill, because I didn't give you fair notice. But next month, Donny, darling, you pay." That's how children learn to manage their money.

I sat for a minute after we hung up the phone. Donny had his first real girlfriend! After I caught my breath, I sent my assistant out to buy every single book she could find on teenage sex. She came back with a bunch of them. When Donny came home for vacation, they were all piled on his bed. I didn't say a word about them. It's hard for me to speak to a boy about kissing and how a man feels romancing a girl and all that. It's actually easier with a younger child, when it's just theory. But when they're coming to "that age," it's a little difficult. I would have no trouble discussing contraception in general terms, but

247

as for the mechanics of it, I think that has to come from a man.

I asked my boyfriend Riccardo to please bring the subject up with Donny. When he next visited he took Donny off for a walk, just the two of them, and they had a man-to-man talk. My friend went into all those things that I wasn't comfortable dealing with. I also asked Riccardo's son to speak with Donny because I knew Donny would relate well to him; he's closer to Donny in age.

I let about a month go by to give him some time to absorb all of this. Then I sat him down and said, "Donny, I know you read the books and spoke to my friends. What do you think of all this?"

He said, "Mom, I knew that stuff all along."

"Oh. Mister Cool. Okay. But there's one thing about which I don't want you to be Mister Cool, and that's protection.

"You cannot—I repeat *cannot*—have sex without protection.

"Now I know this may be premature. You may not be ready to go that far with a girl yet. I want to get to you *before* you have sex. I don't want you to do it even once without protection.

"Because, darling, if you —— without taking precautions, you can die."

I used a very strong word for the sex act and Donny jumped. He wasn't used to hearing such a word from his mother. But it got the result I wanted. He was certainly giving me his fullest attention.

I said, "I'm not just kidding around. This is very serious. You can really truly die from having unprotected sex just once. Don't think you're safe because you're young. You might sleep with a sixteen-year-old girl—but she might sleep with a nineteen-year-old boy, and a nineteen-year-old boy could be sleeping with a twenty-year-old woman—and a twenty-year-old woman . . . who knows who she's sleeping with?

"You have this little sweetheart, and she's holding your hand, and I think it's great. I'm not urging you to move fast. The slower the better, and enjoy every minute along the way. But when the time comes, Donny . . . not even once without a rubber, you hear me? Not *once*.

"Not only don't I want you to get a horrible disease. I also don't want any pregnancies at this time in your life. Remember, this is just your first romance. You're going to university, she's going to university. You'll both have careers. You have a gorgeous life waiting for you. Don't be stupid or careless. Don't mess it up for yourselves."

I recently read an article in the *International Herald Tribune* that said that eighty percent of the women who die of AIDS are between the ages of fifteen and twenty-five. I tore it out and gave it to Donny. I made him read that article—aloud—about a hundred times.

There are those who say we shouldn't talk so openly about contraception to young people, but I don't think you have any choice in this day and age. Your kid's entire future is at stake and I don't see how you can take chances with it.

Kids feel invulnerable, the arrogance of youth. But you have to impress upon them that they're not. *Nobody* is immune. Therefore, the use of condoms is something we don't negotiate.

"No condom, no sex," I tell Donny, and will tell the others when they're old enough. "I don't care how badly you want it. It's better to live to want sex another day."

Our children had the misfortune of being born into a tough time. When I was a teenager, I was an athlete and we weren't allowed to have sex at all—they told us it takes too much out of you and distracts your attention from your sport. Being on the national ski team you can't fall in love, think about the man, miss the man, call the man, instead of practicing. You lose your concentration. So consequently, I didn't have my first boyfriend till I was about eighteen or nineteen. But we were still a luckier generation. If you slept with somebody, maybe you got into trouble, but the price you paid wasn't death.

You'd have to be brain-dead in this day and age to have unrestricted sex. Because now if you make a mistake you can die for it. There was that famous Russian ballet star who knew he had AIDS for eight or ten years before he died—*and didn't tell his sexual partners!* I didn't know him but I have friends who did and they told me he was the most selfish son of a gun you can imagine. He wanted everybody to wait on him but he never did anything for anybody. It was always "Me, me, me. Me the genius, Me the artist, Me on the stage." He may have been a giant talent, I certainly don't dispute that, but as a person he wasn't much. Can you imagine how many people he gave the disease to? There's no excuse for that.

As a mother of children, I find myself terrified. Knowing how teenagers are, I worry about them. Not just AIDS—although it certainly is a horrible, dreadful plague. But drinking and driving, the whole bit. I don't think there are any parents on the face of the earth who aren't afraid for their children.

For myself, I'm not really afraid of anything. I take good care of myself, as much as a person can: Some things, of course, are beyond our control. I'm not afraid of meeting new people, of going new places. I'm a great believer in common sense. I wouldn't go to Harlem at four in the morning, because you're asking for trouble. Nothing about the world really frightens me with the exception of snakes; if I ran across one, I wouldn't freeze or anything, I would just use that common sense I was telling you about . . . and run like hell. But socially, there's very little than can faze me. What's the worst that could happen?

As long as nobody's hurt or bleeding, I'm sure I could still laugh at it. And with that attitude, since people do better when they're not nervous and worried, things tend to turn out okay. I have to share with you a funny story about the time H.R.H. Prince Charles came to visit.

It came about this way. My friend Alecko Papamarkou is also a very good friend of Constantine II, the former king of Greece, who happens to be a buddy of Prince Charles. Alecko was my houseguest in Mar-a-Lago when he got a phone call from Constantine, who at that moment was in a plane en route from Pittsburgh to Palm Beach with Prince Charles for an important polo match. They were staying with another friend of ours, not on the beach.

Anyway, apparently the king had been telling Prince Charles that his friend Alecko Papamarkou was staying with us and Prince Charles mentioned how much he would like to see Mar-a-Lago. So now Constantine was asking Alecko, who asked me, "Is there any possibility that the royal party can drop by for tea?"

Well, you know the answer to that one, and it's not "No." I got the call about four in the afternoon. The prince and his company were due at five so I had one hour in which to pull things together. Mar-a-Lago became a scene of controlled bedlam. One person was doing tea sandwiches, another was baking cookies, yet another was hauling out the gold tea and coffee services.

Wouldn't you know that at that moment, all my houseguests—Aileen Mehle was there and Jerry Zipkin and Kenneth Lane, Baronessa di Portanova, Nan Kempner, and some other people—were out shopping! Not only would they never forgive me, a house looks so much friendlier and so inviting when it's filled with people. I knew everyone was probably out wandering on Worth Avenue, the main shopping street in Palm Beach, so I sent the driver out to find my guests and drag them home—

with strict instructions not to tell them why! Then I called other friends. Estée Lauder told me she never got dressed as fast as she did that day.

My kids were out. Naturally—who spends a sunny Florida afternoon indoors? I sent someone else to find the kids and get them into the house, so they could clean up and change clothes.

My (then) husband was on the golf course. I called the club and told the caddy, "I will give you a hundred dollars if you go find Mr. Trump and tell him to come home immediately. Tell him there's no emergency but he is to come home immediately." I didn't want him to have a heart attack, you see, but I also didn't want him to play just a few more holes. I couldn't tell him directly that Prince Charles was coming to visit because then it would be in the newspapers before the prince could even walk through the door.

In the midst of all this, the police arrived to check out security and so there were police dogs everywhere, officers climbing the palm trees, and helicopters buzzing overhead.

Someone told me later how funny it was when the prince's plane landed in Palm Beach airport. There was the usual crush that surrounds the royal family: police, private security, and, of course, the press corps. The royal party got into limousines, and everybody else was about to follow when suddenly the prince's party made an unexpected turn and disappeared! Even his hostess didn't know where he'd gotten to!

By the time the prince and his retinue arrived at Mar-a-Lago, I had a salon full of people, and the tea and sandwiches and cookies were being passed. Donald was there, my family was there, the houseguests and local crème de la crème were there. People were sipping and nibbling and chatting. It looked for all the world as if this visit had been planned for a year. You'd have *sworn* we'd known about this for longer than sixty minutes.

I may have been panting inwardly, but I looked cool as can be—and so did everyone else. Prince Charles stayed about two hours, and he was extremely gracious. I had about five hundred pictures taken, of my father and my kids with Prince Charles, and he acted as if he were enjoying every minute. I know he really did enjoy looking around Mar-a-Lago because he loves art and architecture.

The whole escapade was fun, and I still smile when I think about it. Especially when I think of the socialite who sent her yacht to Spain *for the whole summer,* just in the hope that on one of his visits the prince might one day come aboard for cocktails. Every hostess in the world would kill to have him—and he just fell into my lap . . . so to speak.

You never know what the day will bring. Of course most of the time it's nothing as exciting as this, or as much fun. But I do try to take it all in my stride and with a spirit of adventure. And I believe I can do that because I don't waste energy stewing over things that are beyond my control. Most of the time I sleep very well at night, and if there are sometimes nights when I have trouble drifting off, it's not because I'm worrying but because I'm excited about something. If I have a big meeting or a big decision to make, I might toss and turn a bit thinking about it, trying to work out a strategy: What will he say, what will she say? I try to foresee what could possibly happen and have answers ready. But once I work out what I have on my mind, I can fall asleep. If I'm facing an adversary I try to think of the worst thing he could do to me, and how I would handle that. I think of possible approaches and answers.

It's like when I'm driving; I never take for granted that the person in the car next to me will stay in his lane. I always think: What if he suddenly shoots out in front of me—and I mentally prepare for it. When I walk on the street, I always know who's behind me. I don't assume that because you're on Fifth Avenue nothing can happen to you. If somebody's breathing down my neck I either go to one side of the street or the other, or I stop and look in a window. If the person goes by, then you know they didn't do it on purpose and it just happened.

I'm always aware, always alert, trying to foresee danger. Common sense together with street smarts are my best assets. And I try very hard to pass them along to my children.

I haven't spoken to Ivanka too much about the facts of life: She's too young. She probably knows that babies are not made by kissing, but I don't think she knows all the technical details yet—at least I hope not. When the time is right, I will sit her down and tell her everything she has to know. Probably next year, and definitely before she goes to Switzerland.

I always believe in giving the emotional side of sex along with the "facts." The plain cold facts are not enough. Relations between men and women, boys and girls, are more than just biological technicalities.

I'm going to tell Ivanka that boys want one thing only, especially when they are young. I'll also tell her that getting pregnant at a young age can ruin her life, and I do not want her under any circumstances to become pregnant (until the right time, of course). I'll share with her that I didn't start my sex life until I was eighteen and she should wait as long as she can. I want her to enjoy her youth—and there will be plenty to enjoy without sex.

I do not want to see her married and a mother while she's still a teenager. "Ivanka, I'm not interested in being a grandmother so fast."

On the other hand, I'll say to her, "Whatever problem you have, come to me right away and tell me about it. If we know the problem, we can solve it together."

I'm trying to raise my children just as my parents raised me because I think they handled it well. They came to me and said, "Ivana, have a boyfriend if you want. But don't get married till after you finish university. At least you will have your education before you start having children. The studying years are the best years of your life, carefree and wonderful. Don't lose them for anything. We would like you to promise us that you won't marry until you finish your studies. That will be time enough for marriage and all it brings with it."

I made that promise to them and I kept it; I've never been sorry. I believe they were very wise and I've asked Ivanka to promise me the same thing.

I tell her, "I enjoy you children and I love you to death, but once you're a mother your carefree days are over. Especially when the kids are small and they have to be around you twenty-four hours a day. Youth is a time to be free and do crazy things and take risks. But once you have a child, parachute jumping is out! You suddenly face responsibility: What will happen to your child if something happens to you? It's a whole other way of thinking.

"Those young years should be the best of your life, and if you get married at eighteen or nineteen you'll miss out and you can never have it again."

But there's only so much a parent can do, and I know it. If it happens that Ivanka comes home one day and says, "I've met somebody wonderful, I want to marry him," I won't have any choice but to support it. I would try to talk her out of it for sure, but if you forbid them, they turn against you and then you have no influence at all. So I'd try to go along with it, while stalling for time.

"How about getting engaged first?" I'd suggest.

I'd also try to work on the boy. I'd take him aside and say, "Ivanka promised me she wouldn't get married until she finishes her education, and it's very important to me. I know you adore her, you make a wonderful couple, so if you want to get engaged, it's all right with me. But let's wait a bit for the wedding, yes? We don't have to plan it just yet. We want to enjoy the engagement to the fullest— the parties, the showers, all that."

This way the children feel they've gotten somewhere. They're engaged, she's got a ring, all her girlfriends are a little jealous. . . . Their wishes are being paid attention to.

But the bottom line to me is that they're *not married*. If it lasts, and they do want to get married later on, fine. If it doesn't, an engagement is easily gotten out of.

It's a good thing that I can smell a fortune hunter from miles away. The boys are going to be after Ivanka in droves. She's beautiful, she's intelligent, and she's not poor. I have to be very cautious that boys won't try to go with her because she's Ivana and Donald Trump's daughter. Ivanka loves children and I know she wants to get married one day and have some. Recently, we were talking about Bon Jovi, the rock star, whom Ivanka adores. We saw an item in the newspaper that he and his wife are expecting their first child. Ivanka said, "But she's only about twenty!"

I said, "There are girls who get married at twenty and if they're married they have children."

Ivanka said, "But isn't that *young?*"

Sometimes, praise God, you get through to them.

Just to give you a roundup of where my kids stand as of this writing, Donny is finishing his third year of boarding school; he's mad about guns and boats, and wavers between wanting to be a Marine and wanting to be a marine architect. As a mother, I'd much prefer he pick a career in which he wouldn't get shot at. Eric at ten is bright, a straight-shooter, and doesn't take no for an answer. He's still very young, but it won't surprise me if he turns out to have a good business head.

My beautiful Ivanka, as you know, is going off to

boarding school in Switzerland in a couple of years to study languages. The school she'll be going to in Switzerland is very strict. They don't allow their students to drive until the age of twenty-one. They said, "None of our children is on drugs. We don't have it in our school."

I said, "Every school has drugs."

It turns out they really don't. They require every child to go once a week for a urine test. If they find something, that child is instantly expelled. No discussion, no mercy. No crying, no explanation, no calls from parents. The child has to leave within twenty-four hours.

I was thrilled. I thought they were brilliant.

Can you believe that some of the parents objected to this? If it required a needle, I could understand it. But here's a cup, go pee-pee in it—and with this small nuisance your child is safe from probably the biggest plague of our time. I say, do it! What's more important, a little embarrassment or knowing if your kid is on drugs?

I sat each of my kids down and promised them that if they don't smoke, take drugs, or drink alcohol until they reach driving age, I will buy each of them a car. But one cigarette, and it's all over. Let's face it, I'll probably have to buy them a car anyway, but this way I'm getting something for it. And I'm giving them time to develop some common sense and get some control over those raging teenage hormones. In today's society, if you can make sure your kids don't lie, cheat, or steal, and if they don't take drugs or abuse alcohol, that's probably the best you can do. And the only way I know to make that happen is to talk, talk, talk to your kids. Because they're getting so much input from the other side.

Your kids want to be cool—*all* kids want to be cool. Their friends are having a beer, they'll have a beer. Then they drive, and the next one is driving like a crazy person, so they have to try it too. There are so many influences, and if you don't talk to them, you have no idea what's going on. Goodness knows they know more than we ever did. Who *knows* what they see on those cable stations?

You don't want them to get the idea that the entire relationship between men and women boils down to the rubbing of body parts. But I believe that kind of teaching starts long before your child is ready for his first girlfriend or her first boyfriend. It starts in infancy. The children learn just by watching you, and your marriage. If you are a lady, they see the way you deal with people and the way you are treated.

If you and your husband are divorced, chances are there isn't too much opportunity for your son to observe his father and you being gentle and sweet and loving with each other. You don't want your son to grow up treating girls (and later women) in an uncaring way.

There are two separate areas I think you have to be concerned with for boys. One is manners, etiquette. If the men in your life tend to slam the car door and walk away, you don't want your son to copy the people around him. You can't depend on him to learn the right way to behave just from observation, you have to do some real tutoring.

Sit him down and go through the basics: "Darling, when you get out of a car, go around and open her door. When you go to a restaurant, let the lady sit first. Then you go around the table and sit down.

"Try to let her start to eat first before you gobble up the hamburger. If you see she's finished her soda, ask her if she wants another one.

"Don't just drop the girl at the curb, walk her all the way inside and open the door for her; make sure she's safe. Be a gentleman."

From the time they could toddle into a room, I taught my kids to say hello if someone is with me. They have to greet the other person, then they can say whatever it is they want to say.

I think all of us who are mothers of sons have an obligation to teach them more than just basic etiquette; we have to teach them how to treat women. They have to be decent in their relationships, and when a girl says no, it means no. Period. I'd like to see the term "date rape" disappear from our vocabularies, and I think we mothers of sons can do something to help that come about.

You may wonder why I'm focusing on boys. Of course girls need to have nice manners too, and they need to be kind and decent with the opposite sex. However, girls seem to come by their manners much more naturally and easily. Somehow they learn to eat nicely and neatly, to follow the general rules of etiquette. They're just much more social.

As far as the second point, I worry far more about what men do to women than what women do to men. I can't help it. I'm a woman—I see that side more clearly. But even realistically, I think men do more damage to women than women to men. Men have the money and the power and the *drive* to be dominant. When was the last time you heard of a case of date rape where *she* forced *him* to have sex?

All my three kids were conceived with protection. I don't know how it happened. I hated every minute of every pregnancy. You lose your body, you look like a whale. When the first one turned out to be a boy, I said, "Great. I'm done."

I became pregnant again. It was a girl. A boy and a girl. Now I'm surely done.

Then came Eric, my baby—and he is *really* the last.

After Eric was born, I said, "I'm closing the shop." I used multiple contraception. There was no way I could conceive again.

Make no mistake, much as I hated the process, I love the product. I'm very close to my kids. We have fun together; we travel together, do sports, picnic, hike, scuba dive, swim. At the age of two I took each of them to the top of a hill and told them, "Ski down."

They would wail, "I don't like it."

"Tough, honey," I'd tell them. "Get to the bottom of the mountain."

Donny and Ivanka weren't too bad, but Eric would cry for hours at a time. I'd give him to the ski instructor and say, "Don't worry if he cries. He'll get over it. He's got to learn."

Poor little Eric would be skiing and crying at the same time: "I want to go home!" The instructor would tell him, "If I take you home I'll get fired. I have a kid like you, I have to support that kid."

But you see, when he finally stopped falling and started getting a little bit of control, he liked the way it felt, and now Eric can't wait to hit the slopes.

All my kids love to ski. Skiing is movement, speed, danger, wind, incredible freedom. They adore it, as I do. We're a skiing family.

My kids have had every pet there is except cats. Cats shed and they're unpredictable and they scratch. But we have two dogs, fish, birds in every room, turtles, mice—name it, we've got it. I find it so funny that children adore hamsters—they're rodents, that's all they are. The kids brought home a little white mouse, a school pet, at the end of the school year, and they begged, "Mom, can we keep it?"

I told them that we'd keep mice in Trump Tower over my dead body, but if they promised they'd take it to Greenwich and keep it *outside* the house, in the garage somewhere, and if *they'd* feed it and take care of it, and I'd never *see* it or play with it or touch it . . . it was all right with me.

The kids kept the mouse. It had a cage with straw on the bottom and a little mouse playhouse. Sure enough, about fourteen days later, the kids came running in with the cage. There were a dozen little mousies inside, each one only the size of a fingernail; pink skin and no hair. They looked so ghastly, I almost had a heart attack.

I said, "I'm going to die. Do something! Give them to the zoo. God forbid one mouse gets free; I'm going to be chasing white mice around the house for the rest of my life!"

A duck, now, that's a pet. I was walking on the road outside our home in Greenwich and I found a duck that had been hurt in the head. It probably collided with something. I took it home and the kids named it Wobbly, because it wobbled around so. I think it was dizzy. We nursed it back to health. Wobbly lived in the bathtub, but he followed us around wherever we went. We tried to bring him to the ocean to teach him to swim, but Wobbly didn't want to go in the ocean, he wanted to come with us. We'd set him down, point him in the right direction. He would fly a little bit and come right back to us. Finally, we gave him to one of the men who worked on the property. He slowly taught Wobbly to be free. I hope he's all right.

One day I was walking along the road with Ivanka, and we saw this gorgeous animal come out of the woods. Large, dark eyes, silky coat. It turned around, showing its back to us, lifting its tail . . .

I yelled, "Ivanka—run!"

Ivanka and I took off. I had realized—just in time—that it was a skunk . . . a *frightened* skunk, about to let loose. One of our dogs got sprayed by a skunk, and it was unbearable. I called the vet, he said to bathe the animal in two gallons of tomato juice. So we dipped the poor dog in tomato juice—and if you think he wanted to take that bath in tomato juice, you are wrong.

As you can probably tell, I adore my kids.

I always say I'm like that American Express commercial, I never leave home without them.

Chapter 13

Your New Life Will Be Better than the Old One

I can't stress enough that how well you come through your divorce depends almost entirely on how you look at it. If you think of it as a beginning rather than an ending, an opportunity rather than a tragedy, another chance, another chapter in the adventure of your life, you'll be fine.

This postdivorce time is a good time to stretch mentally as well as physically. If there was ever anything you wanted to learn or do or try, now's the time to do it.

Take a risk or two. What can you lose?

What's the worst that could happen? You'll be embarrassed? You don't die of embarrassment. Honest. If you're too sensitive and self-conscious, I think you need to work at cultivating a thicker skin. You can miss out on an awful lot by being afraid to dare.

I'm not easily thrown, even by obvious viciousness.

I remember once when my ex-husband and I were still married and we were invited by a very prominent, very wealthy, and very nasty woman to her place on Park Avenue for a black-tie dinner. I think I looked pretty nice. I had a beautiful gown, some jewelry; my hair and makeup were done. When I came in front of her on the receiving line, the woman looked me up and down and said, "You look good. For an immigrant."

"I take that as a compliment," I told her.

Ask yourself, who do you think badly of in the story I just told you? *She* was trying to embarrass *me*, but it didn't work, did it? Dreadful people usually wind up making fools of *themselves*.

Thankfully there aren't too many terrible people out there. In all likelihood you won't encounter anyone nearly as awful. But what I want you to understand is, even if the worst happens, you'll live.

If you can only believe that—really, truly accept it— you won't be self-conscious anymore. It's very liberating.

I happen to think that moving easily and gracefully among people is a skill. And like any skill, you can improve with practice.

You have to do your homework, so that when you're with people the conversational ball won't drop with you. I read a lot; about two books a month, and all the newspapers and magazines I can find—and that's a lot: business magazines, fashion magazines, sports magazines, and some technical magazines.

I'm not saying you have to be a rocket scientist in everything. You don't. But you do have to have a general awareness of what's happening around you. When I go to a dinner, I don't care who the hostess sits me next to, I know I'll be able to make conversation. I know someone who never gives a dinner unless it has a business or social purpose. It's never just to entertain her friends, there's always something she's trying to get out of it. That I don't like. But otherwise, sit me next to anybody, I don't care. I'll do my best to make it work. There's always something I'd like to know and by the end of the evening I try to have learned something.

If I'm seated next to a heart specialist, let's say, I try to get a little knowledge out of him about his work. It doesn't have to be a doctor, it could be a coal miner. I say, "That's very interesting. Tell me about it."

Of course they ask me about myself; they want to be entertained too. Usually I'm seated next to businesspeople, and I try to stay up on the currencies, the European markets, the global situation. People feel more comfortable when they're talking about something they know, so I ask lots of questions: How is that? How did it happen?

And you just listen and take it all in like a sponge. That's how you get smart.

I'm one person you can't accuse of idle dreaming, because all my dreams have come true. But I did more than sit around and daydream.

I wish I could take each of you for a cup of tea, and we could sit together and work out your problems. Since I can't, I wrote this book. I want to assure you with all my heart that the techniques I've described here work.

I know what you're feeling.

I know how hopeless you can feel at times. You write me letters and tell me in person as I travel around the country. I truly, truly believe that as long as there's life, there's hope. I want you to look at your strengths in the same way I did. Literally count them, make a list of them. And then think of imaginative ways to put those strengths to work.

I'll help with a few suggestions to start you off, and I'll bet you think of more.

You're lonely? Teach someone to read and your spirits will lift, I promise you. Check the local school and library. Many of them need volunteers to teach literacy.

Is there a home for the aged nearby that could use a

cheerful visitor? Hook up with an organization like Meals on Wheels—they deliver ten thousand meals a day to shut-ins, invalids, the elderly, etc., and they always need people. Often the person from Meals on Wheels is the only human contact that a shut-in will have that day. You'll make a tremendous difference in other people's lives, you'll be doing something absolutely wonderful for another human being—and that will give you such a good feeling about yourself!

Don't tell me there's nothing you can do. I won't believe it. Everybody loves your baking? Check with the restaurants and cafés near your home. Many of them would happily order trays of home-baked goodies. You could have a small business going.

I'm a firm believer in putting your skills to work for you. If you can sew well, perhaps you want to take a class to get even better and do it as a professional.

You like to cook? Get a job in the kitchen of a restaurant or large hotel. At first you'll be chopping vegetables and stirring things, but you'll be getting paid and I'm convinced that you can work your way up. I heard of one woman who had to stay home with her small children. But she could make these delightful meat pastries. She baked up a tray and left her children with a neighbor for a few hours and took samples around to the local bakeries. They placed orders!

Another woman has a small sideline going in fancy cakes for birthdays and holidays. Not the society wedding cakes that cost thousands but affordable birthday cakes with little figurines on them that children like so much. Her birthday cakes are such a hit she has no trouble selling the gingerbread houses she makes at Christmas by special order. She uses wonderful ingredients and her cakes are expensive, but not astronomically so. When she has nothing to do on a Sunday, she'll bake up a few and decorate them according to the season. She makes some phone calls and invariably finds people who want them.

Perhaps you've got a green thumb. Ask at a local nursery if they can use you. Even if you can't do heavy physical labor, they always need people to walk around talking to the customers about plants.

If you can clean house well, a good hotel would love to have you. Big hotels are always looking for housekeepers. When I ran the Plaza Hotel in New York City, we needed maids constantly, and at busy times we needed extra people who could work part-time. You don't need degrees or previous experience for a job like that. All you have to do is work hard and carefully. When we found a woman who did her work well, after a while we'd put her in charge of a guest floor. A year later she might be a supervisor, and in five years head of housekeeping. If it were me, at that point the head of the department should be looking to his or her job, because I'd be after it.

Yes, I think big. So should you. That's what this book is all about.

Whatever it is you do, do it well and do it with joy. The best is yet to come. I believe that with all my heart— and I've got a pillow on my couch that says so, in case I'm ever tempted to forget.

I'm not one who tells people that when bad things happen it's all to the good—sometimes that can be really unrealistic. But I do know that going through a divorce can change your life in many ways. If you take control, plan well, and use your strengths, I think those changes can be for the better.

I know I'm asking you to do this at a time when you feel about as big as the dot at the end of this sentence. In the eyes of many people you've probably lost a lot of position and prestige by no longer being Mrs.-who-you-were. A columnist once said: "Ex-wives count for less than zero. They disappear."

I didn't accept that. And I won't allow you to.

This is really the time for you to blossom and go in directions you never dreamed of. Often, men think that when they divorce you (or you divorce them) you will lie down and die. When that doesn't happen, they can become very nasty. They simply can't believe it: She dares to go and live her life and be happy? It makes them jealous. After all, they owned you and therefore when they drop you, you should break. But you know the saying, behind every successful woman there is a man in shock.

> I'm sure that the "empire" would have developed a lot differently had Donald been married to a selfish or troublesome woman. You were an asset to him. Now please be an asset to yourself.
>
> Pearl

As I told you, when my husband and I separated, I began to suspect my days as president of the Plaza Hotel were numbered. Not only did I accept that, I welcomed it. It was a fabulous job and I enjoyed every minute of it, but when it was over, it was over. I could easily have stayed in hotel management. Believe me, I got more than one offer. I am very proud of what I achieved as president of the Plaza Hotel. After I had run it for little over a year, we were named the seventh-best luxury hotel in the world by *Travelers* magazine. There were only two other American hotels in the same category. *Pinnacle* magazine named us the best hotel in North America for corporate meetings, banquet space, and conventions. *Prestige* magazine named us the most improved. *Worth* magazine named me the Hotelier of the Year—and that honor was voted by my peers in the industry! You know how much I treasure that!

I could have accepted any one of the offers that was made to me, but I decided to stay away from anything that was connected to my previous life.

We separated in February and I stayed in the Plaza until June.

I left and I never looked back.

Now I'm doing some things I always wanted to do. I have a new phase in my life, and new careers. I have a calendar full of speaking engagements around the country. I'm producing skin care products—something I've always had a yen for. I wanted to write—well, I did, two novels and this book. My first novel, *For Love Alone,* was a *New York Times* best-seller, and CBS aired a TV miniseries of my second book, *Free to Love*; videos of the film are being sold all over the world. I love designing clothes and jewelry and putting together outfits that a woman of average means will be able to buy and enjoy. I appear with them on the Home Shopping Network once a month.

You have to know what you want, be determined to get it—and be willing to work like the devil. A woman wrote me that she had been married for fifteen years before her divorce. She called herself "an ordinary housewife." Her divorce settlement left her fairly well off and she decided this was her chance to do what she'd always wanted, to go to medical school. She wasn't as young as some, she certainly wasn't carefree. But she *is* a practicing physician today. She took her settlement money, got out of the house, went to school . . . and fulfilled a dream.

That's what I want for you.

Dream big dreams. And make them come true.

Sigmund Freud once said: "Despite my thirty years of research into the feminine soul, I have not yet been able to answer the great question: What does a woman want?"

Well, I can answer that for you, Dr. Freud. A woman wants exactly what a man wants: to fulfill her potential.

I challenge all of you, if you want to reach your full potential, to answer these questions:

What do you want?

What are your goals?

What do you dare to do to turn your dreams into reality?

I hope that some of the ideas I have shared with you will motivate you to keep reaching for your dreams.

I also hope that you now have a glimpse of me that goes beyond the image portrayed in the media. The love of my parents, my children, and friends has helped me enormously, but I have learned that without my personal conviction and faith in myself, I could not have survived these difficult times.

I believe that within all of us are the seeds of success. They have to be nurtured and nourished, but they're there, just waiting to bring you all that you wished for and dreamed of.

Eleanor Roosevelt said, "A woman is like a tea bag. You never know how strong she is until she gets into hot water."

The best is yet to come. Remember that.